A DIFFERENT WICKET!

THROUGH THE PAGES OF LIFE

SAJID QAMAR

ISBN 979-888521805-4

To Abba ,Ammi,my family members,friends ,Nazia,Maaz ,Maira and Narita (my student) who all have made me push my limitation, in whatever the little I have managed to do through this book.

Contents

About The Author   vii

PART I

1. At Threshold   3

2. Our Wanton Days   13

3. The Ball, Set In Motion   16

4. Gathering Moss   19

5. New Awakening   40

6. An Epoch Making   47

7. Throwing The Dice   54

8. Home Calling   59

PART II

9. A Different Ball Game   67

10. A Whirlwind   90

11. Lessons Learnt   98

About The Author

Dr.Sajid Qamar was born at Hazaribagh.He did his Masters from Vinoba Bhave University.He was awarded his Ph.D degree in 2018.His topic of the research was 'Kamala Das -As an Iconoclast:A Critical Evaluation Of Her Major Prose Works'.He has been teaching English Language and Literature in Holy Cross School for twenty years.

PART I

CHAPTER ONE

AT THRESHOLD

I could not see my hands and I was extremely frightened, as there would not be enough light at Kallu chowk. I was dropped there by our team manager, Mr.Mallick. It was around 2:30 of the morning. I was getting back from Dhanbad after playing Inter-district match. After every step I would stop and look around. Even the creaking sound of the shoes was terrifying. I was placing every step very cautiously to avoid any sound. My kit bag and travel bag were making it all the more difficult to move swiftly. I was hardly a few hundred meters away from my home but it proved to be of many kilometers. I was in ninth std. and till then I had nothing substantial to say about my achievement in cricket. An unguided passion was forcing me towards the game. A silent introspection could have worked. But even for that a pep talk, an interactive session with experts or proper counselling was needed.

In those days there were not so many people with good knowledge of career counselling. People like dim-municipal- light would show us path with whatever the little light they had. My Father used to be the mast-light for all kind of guidance.

Now when I think about those moments I find that the darkness was not because of the absence of light but it was the absence of the right direction. Setting goal, putting in effort are common to all who test their hands in sports, music, art etc. But the recipe of success needs some more ingredients like, fearlessness in taking chance, Knowing ones' strength and weakness, timing etc. They don't come to people like auto-fill content. They come with counselling, introspection and guidance. These aforesaid elements develop an approach which enables a person to withstand all the emotional jolts and jerks one receives on the way of success.

Failure teaches us more than success. But this teaching is only possible when we are ready to accept the failure. History tells us that failure did not stop all the successful people, whose names are 'glittering stars' on the pages of history, from making attempt with the better understanding, caused by a careful analysis of the same. This, they did by changing their angle of viewing at the things. For such people **END** means, Effort Never Dies, **NO** means, Next Opportunity and **FAIL** means, First Attempt In Learning. These people also proved that water or rain makes people change their cloth but when sweat makes people change their cloth , such people change the world.

Life is like a Test cricket in which we get to bat in the second inning at different wickets, after failing to do something useful for the team in the first. Because we always have some idea about the wicket. However each challenge, thrown by life, is like a new ball, bowled by a bowler. The first inning of every individual remains events packed. It starts from the childhood which includes schooling till primary level. This is the most beautiful period of one's life. In this period a child believes in whatever he or she sees around. They don't have the ability to choose friends .Their innocence gets reflected through their action and behavior. The very behavior paves way to shape their character, the environment they find themselves in .Now the character of the parents becomes an integral part of a child's personality and views. Here a child is like a sapling who needs the best of cares of their parents. Parents ought to be careful about the opinion they mouth about their wards in front of them. Like, 'you are stupid', 'you can't do anything properly' 'Grow up now' etc. are some very common remark, passed on by parents. Things become all the more critical when parents make comparison in front of other siblings. It is easy to turn a child away but very difficult to convince them. Lecture and admonishment don't do any good to them, but in order to create quality in them parents will have to set their examples by implementing the desired values in their life. As children have the quality of copying, by birth. It goes without saying that the Good they see in their parents they imbibe them without being told. Many parents consider their wards to be incapable. They use words like idiot, lazy, nonsense etc. for them. This shatters the belief system of their wards. After shattering their confidence they expect their ward to win the confidence of others. Then there takes place a fight within the child. Fighting their lone battle they grow up. Now they are in the secondary level they have other source to get information from. Today media especially the social media which may include some games, should be given credit for shaping the thoughts and ideas in the young minds. They do it so repeatedly that the contents vomited by them become a part of their belief system. By the time they reach the senior secondary level their friends and people who are very close, influence them as they have the relationship of trust with them. Incidences, events, and experiences also contribute in their belief system, even though some (events and incidences) of them are not in their control. Teachers also play an important role in their success. Some time they find their ideal in them and their words of encouragement are certificates for them. Teachers can make an incapable students believe that they are capable. A teacher does not realize how and when they move their brush and give a shade of belief to the personality of the students.

My first inning has an average kind of beginning to the standard of early eighties. When I walk down in memory lane I find my mohallah, blanketed by darkness as electricity was a mercy at the hands of the Electricity Department. Electricity poles had been tired of bearing the burden of the bulbs which had forgotten how to give light. The time of LED was still many decades away. Electricity, playing hide and seek was order of the day. We had to rely on lantern, lamp or home-made light called 'dhibri' for our studies. The setting of the sun was an understood call for all of us to get back home and study. The importance of Khaki clad person, called postman was known to all. A letter was an inevitable part of emotional self. There came a time when few houses had a landline phone. All the important national calls or some international calls of the people of mohallah, came there only. They showed great deal of humility and sincerity in making people receive their call even in the night. Television was an alien to most of us. When we heard about a machine named 'television' for the first time, we friends formed all imaginative ideas about it. Even Some of us would guess that we would be able to see each other in their houses through that machine. The advent of television was no doubt an epoch making event in our life. We were lost in the entertainment, not known earlier. Its impact gradually crept in our lifestyle. Serial like Malgudi Days, Mahabharat, Karamchand 'Star-Trek', He-Man, Battle of the Planets etc, also used to push the horizon of our imagination. In fact ours was the generation which was witnessing the biggest transition in the human history. Television had made entry in our life and 'computer', the greatest invention after fire and wheel, was knocking our doors. We were to experience an unimaginable change in all walks of our life.

I grew up seeing a struggling but a resolute father. He took lots of pride in talking about his father and my grandfather, Syed Abdul Ghafoor,a freedom fighter from Zila School ,Hazaribagh, who was jailed and tortured wherein during Non-Cooperation Movement. My father often quoted him as saying, "The One who has given for body will give for shroud". He never played cricket but took interest when India played against any country. He was all praise for Sunil Gavaskar. About contemporary cricketers, he used to call them arrogant especially when they lost a match.

One evening there came a few cars in front of my house. In those days any four wheeler pulled the attention of all those who were around because it was not seen quite often. My father was in .Having heard the knocking at the gate I came out to see. I saw a few khadi clad people, with a bag in one's hand. I informed my father. He entertained them in the front room which faced the main entrance. I being the youngest male member of the family served them tea. After some time they went back.

Next day my mother informed my father that there was no flour at home and therefore he was served rice and pickle. I found him smiling. In those days salary in the minority school was like rainfall in the arid zone and we were quite used to it. That was the testing time for my father. We never found our father getting late for his school. My mother often said, "Why are you so punctual when you are not paid regularly. Others (teachers of the school) don't bother about the timing of the school."

"I don't have to feed my children from the earnings through unfair means. I have to do my duty what I am accountable and paid for," my father replied. After years we came to know that the people, who had come with the bag, were there to offer money to my father for a vote which my father could have given to their candidate, as a ward- commissioner, to become chairman of the Municipal Corporation. In that difficult situation turning down such an offer needed rock solid belief in Almighty and inner strength. The very belief enabled him no to compromise with the quality of the person who would serve the society.

I learnt the importance of humanity and friendship from my father. His life was the example of how to maintain friendship even at the cost of his own well- being. He made us feel that good friends stay with a person. If one doesn't have good friends, it means one lacks the ability to display genuine emotions for them. If the factors contribute, in the decision to make friends, are support and favor of any kind, and if these are the nucleus of any relationship then it becomes purpose- based. It has a well-defined life span. Its root may be traced back to theory of utility. It suggests that when utility of a person ends the relationship ends. Devoid of any genuine emotion in the relationship, it proves to be a purposeful contract. But if selflessness begets a relationship, it thrives in all ups and downs of life. There are people who may not have bank balance but their social balance is great. Such people are social genius. This social bank stops their emotional erosion. This emotional erosion starts faster, the moment a person reaches his superannuation. They might be an officer of high rank and have a herd of yes-men around but now in the evening of life they need somebody who should sit with them and talk. Solitude stares at them and asks about those people who were like their shadow during their heyday .People with social balance don't feel this sudden shift in the position after the retirement. They maintain a very good relationship with people of all class. They are good to an auto driver, plumber, electrician, painter, driver and their own friends. But there are people who run after mundane glory(power and pelf) as if there is a dog after them and when they reach at their desired destination they find themselves far away from all those good people like family members ,childhood friends, and some sometimes even neighbors, who were selflessly attached with them. Such people don't have social balance for the evening of their life.

To complain is a natural act of humans. If there is a bright sunny day then there is a complaint about the sunlight, if there is incessant rain then there is complaint of rain etc. There are so many who pick all the negative news from the newspaper or news channels in the morning and keep discussing all day long with their friends at different places including their dining table, engaging their family members. They are always filled with negativity .They keep spewing the same negativity on others. My father never complained of the issues he had in his life. He faced them head-on with unshakeable belief in Almighty. Robert H. Schuller rightly says, "Tough times never last, but tough people do."

Man is a social animal. He can't live alone. This is the reason they develop relationship, which results in the formation of society and family. A man develops different relationship e.g with wife, friends ,people in the society,at different places, except some, rest are made by God. A person leads all his life, keeping the views and interest of those relationship. Here he fails to understand his own inner and deep seated desire. Pabalo Naruda, a Chilian poet, offers a solution in his poem Keeping Quiet, by asking his readers to do silent introspection.

If we were not so single minded
About keeping our lives moving,
And for once could do nothing
Perhaps this huge silence
Might interrupt this sadness
Of never understanding ourselves
And of threatening ourselves with death.

Today in this socially and scientifically advanced age a new fear, FOMO, fear of missing out, has crept-in in our society. Relationships are forgotten when they don't suit to the need of the people. This happens because we don't check the compatibility of the relationship. In-order to have strong bond or relationship the following points are to be kept in mind-

1. Relationship should be based on genuine feelings and having tendency to do good to others.

2. Always respect those who are close to you.

3. Know the preferences of your friends and make your preferences clear to them.

4. Be transparent in money matters.

5. Don't expect anything but if you are capable, do good to them.

6. Always carry a good smile on your face.

Example is better than precept. I would realize it, day in and day out .When it comes to building selfless relationship I grew up seeing my father, having friends around, whose match are rare today. One such was Usman Uncle. Once my father narrated an incidence about him. He said, "We were going to Aasansol with the baraat of Usmaan bhai. On the way we stopped near a hotel to have some refreshment. I got down and took a jug, on the table, and started drinking water. The owner saw me and started hurling abusive words on me ,I could not control and gave couple of punches to that man. Then the situation took a serious turn. Locals from near-by shops gheroed me and started beating. Somehow the information reached to Usman bhai .He was in the other vehicle. He, having thrown his bridal turban(pagdi)jumped into that crowd and started giving punches to those who had brought me down on the ground. Seeing him the whole baraat party, except women and children, got into the fight. The locals, seeing the tide turning, ran away from there. The seniors from both the party pacified the issue. The owner of the hotel apologized." Father was smiled while narrating. He had many exclamatory sentences for those golden periods when relationship had a great value.

The society ,which ignores their elders, has to face lots of difficulties in dealing with the worldly affairs. This is very apparent in the present society that the time when our elders are loaded with wisdom, we stop talking to them. We consider them and their ideas outdated. It is rightly said, **"The home which does not consider the advices of the elders, it has to take advice from the lawyers."**

Spending time, listening to elders, make us see those hidden aspects of life which, otherwise, we can neither understand nor get exposed to them. We don't have the culture of literary gathering where the richness of literature of different language is discussed. In England there used to be 'coffee houses' where literati used to discuss the subtle points of literature, being the true reflector of the society, which paved the way for many great classics which are still glittering on the firmament of English literature. 'Adda' in Bengal, played somewhat similar role in making the literary mind of the people fertile. People associated with it contributed a lot to the Bangla as well as English literature.

CHAPTER TWO

OUR WANTON DAYS

We friends too gathered at different time at different places. One such place was the campus of Inderpuri Cinema Hall. There was a moment we had to run away from there as somebody had called police for gathering there. But ours was entirely different to that of literary ones. Ours included planning about matches (cricket and football) to be played next day, Comments on the performance in the matches played the previous day, Expert comments on the individual performance of the Indian cricket team(moreover most of the people in our society , however least they know about cricket they confidently comment on the comments, made by the experts who have played for their country).We also shared our day today experience. Our meeting actually did not serve any big purpose. But we did it religiously.

We hardly discussed our career plan. We were studying just for the sake of studying. Our preparation started couple of months before the exam. We had two syllabi one given by university and the other, twelve or thirteen questions with answers printed in the Sharma Guess paper, which was a must have study material for majority of the students. In fact career strategy, planning etc. were not the part of our growing up. Therefore our routine was packed with playing activities. This playing had variety of forms .Swimming in the jheel and plucking guavas and stuffing them into the tucked shirt, while getting back to home. Black berries, wood apple(beil) were other attractions for us.We heard about Some who were very early risers. They got up early and took rickshaw, stood near footpath, and roamed around the town, doing all kind of mischiefs. Burning crackers near the ears of the sleeping rickshaw pullers, sprinkling dry colours on the head of the hotel staff, who slept outside their hotel and other who slept on the foot-path. They realised the colour only while bathing. These didn't stop here. They often went near PTC ground, in those days it had not been fenced, when people ,mostly rickshaw pullers, came for their natural call .There was no water therefore they carried a small jar or bottle for water. These jars or bottles were target for them. When those poor people noticed the danger lurking over their jar or bottle they tried to hide or shift their place in the mid-way of their business, but it would be rather difficult. They, having seen the fallen jar or bottle, lost all hope for getting water, chased those champions, lifting their lungees, emptying all their stock of abuses, that too in their full throat. They would derive lots of pleasure while narrating their mischief. They were least concerned how they were becoming the reason for the mental as well as physical pain of those poor people. Their energy would have reached them to height of success, had that been used in the right direction.

The span of childhood was long in our time. Therefore we could get away with all those reckless acts which would cause laughter to us and sometime pain for others. We didn't take pain to think about the possibilities of serious consequences of those acts.Fun and frolic was something we always aimed at. We were not exposed to the latest technology the way our present generation has been. And this has resulted in the shortening of their childhood span. Ours was the generation which would look at the logo of 'Doordarshan' appear on the television screen with the monotonous background music, with excitement. Some of us didn't leave even Kirshi Darshan, meant for the farmer. Sunday was much more than Sunday of today's time .Mahabharat ,Ek Do Teen Chaar, Tom and Jerry shows ,Charlie Chaplin shows etc used to make each Sunday ,the most awaited day.

CHAPTER THREE

THE BALL, SET IN MOTION

Cricket came to us naturally as the popularity of the game had gripped the whole nation in 1983 when India won Prudential World Cup under the captainship of Kapil Dev.This was a classic example of how 'team-work, leadership from the front, putting in the best without bothering about the result. Picture of Kapil Dev holding the world cup ,with broad smile was almost every-where. Since then cricket in India has never seen back. Young generation had nothing other than cricket. In 1984 Mrs. Indira Gandhi was assassinated and to watch her cremation, which was a live telecast, there was a rush for the television. But it was still not that common in small town like Hazaribagh. Gradually the very advent of Television triggered off the passion for cricket ,in the young generation. Over the decades its radiation has eclipsed all other sports. Cricketers have always had a lion share when it comes to celebrity status in our country.

I was one of the so many kids who had made a bat out the base of a cot. In the free time we could not think any game other than cricket. We used to play inter-mohallah cricket with lots of enthusiasm. In one such match at Zila School Ground, a very senior cricketer Mr. Rajendra watched me play, by then he had already played for state. I scored fifty odd runs in that match. He called me and appreciated my batting. His appreciation filled me with extra passion for cricket. I started my formal cricket with Metropolitan club where Razi bhai was my captain. After few years when the club was closed I switched over to Sporting Union club and remained there till I left cricket.

During our time the obsession for cricket was at its pinnacle. Everyone who held bat wanted to play for country. But I must say that all the aspirants whom I played with, did justice with their effort. Unfortunately, to the best of my knowledge, most of them could not make it to the level where they would make their living comfortably. Consequently we were never encouraged to play cricket .We were often given example of all those cricketers who, having spent their prime of life, returned getting disillusioned ,to doing something to make their living. By then they were strugglers whose energy, will-to-do something new, hope and aspiration had been sucked by cricket. This happened in every nook and corner of the country. In the said situation playing cricket to make career was swimming against the tide. This was not possible without the support of the parents. I was lucky that I got that support from my father although my mother always objected to my playing cricket.

She always said, "What did you get from cricket. Look at yourself your bone is peeping through your body."

"Let me play some more .I will get chance to play at higher level which will enable me to get a job." I replied .My mother's only concern was my health .She was least bothered about selection as she had no idea whatsoever, how a cricketer reaches to the top. I played for Hazaribagh district for many years in all different categories: U-13, U-15, U-17-U-19 and Heymon Trophy. I played well but perhaps I was not good enough for the elite level.

Before achieving success and happiness our mind has to go through a series of negotiations which take place in the formation of our belief system. Before getting approval for our talent and ability by the world, we need to get the same, from within, for our success. We should put our hand on our heart and ask whether we really deserve it. Without self-approval, public- approval is impossible. There should be solid confidence within us for our ability and then we should strive for our goal. As our belief system influence our thoughts and actions,we can't bring about any change in the system without working on the thought process. The very system commands our actions, later resulting in the achievement of the set goal. I personally feel most of the cricketers, from the small town, of our time, had the required ability but they lagged behind in the belief system. Hence they could not do much what they could have done.

Even though cricket didn't give me much in terms of return, what people expect and talk about, I got chance to see life from different perspective .Every cricket tour was important for me as they unfolded layers of life. Staying together, sharing joy of winning and pain and disappointment of losing, helping each other to stand after falling, in terms of performance. An unsaid competition with the teammates ,not at the cost of teams' overall performance ,to get selected for the state team, was always there.

CHAPTER FOUR

GATHERING MOSS

One such tour was to Jamshedpur in the month of June .The kind of heat we experienced, one can use any adjective to describe the intensity. We felt more because at Hazaribagh the mercury never soared that high. Whenever we had a match against a strong opponent like Jamshedpur, Ranchi etc. we had to face two opponents simultaneously, one, which was self-created because of their playing gears and their outfits etc. We used to get impressed by everything they did. Their brandishing of English willow bat with headphone, their match goggles etc. Most of us were from Hindi medium. Co-education was a wonder for us. We were accommodated in DBMS school. Summer vacation had started but students used to be there for official works. Girls students were also there in their shorts and T-shirt. Some of us were craning out our head to have a glimpse of those students as if they were the seventh wonder. We had a team meeting after the dinner. In the meeting some common points were made by the coach and manager. Then we were asked to go to bed and switch off the light. Since we were dead tired we fell on the bed and slept. Some of us were snorting loudly. But who cared! It must be 3:00 or 3:30 in the morning .There was no light in the room.

A big ventilator was serving the purpose. Street light was coming through it. We were sleeping on the carpet with our kit bag on one side. Just then I woke up by some whispering .I saw two shadows were leaning over somebody .I pretended to be as sleeping. When I gazed I found one of them had something like small colgate tube and they were over the groin of that boy.I kept quite. They were giggling and talking to each other. After some time they got back to their places. At around 6:00 I woke up ,hearing the shouting with lots of abusive words. I saw, it was Monoj who had kept both of his hands on his private area and was almost in tears. I jumped up and took Monoj aside.

"What happened?" I said. He was in pain.

"Come with me," He said beckoning me towards the bathroom. By then all the team mates had woken up. The coach and manager, who were there in the adjacent room ,had come. Monoj took me to the bathroom and showed me his groin where I notice some paste like substance had been applied and now that had dried up. It is very painful when we have a paste or gel on the hairy part of our body and dries up.

"Put water there and rub gently," I said. He did and I noticed a tooth paste like sud was there. He rubbed for some time and gradually all the suds disappeared.

"How do you feel now?" I said.

"It's ok, feeling better,"Monoj said.

It was almost time to get ready for the match. When I and Monoj reached room there was silence all around. Some of the players had gone to bathe. Some were arranging their kit bags.

"What happened Monoj?," Amolkant said innocently. Monoj stared at him.

"Tell me yaar what happened,?Amolkant repeatd.

"You bastard ,I know you people have done it.Let me have an opportunity I will not spare any one of you.I will see you at Hazaribagh,"Monoj's reply sounded as if his pent up feeling had been vented. He wanted to speak more but I calmed him down.

"Let's get ready for the match,"I said patting at his back. The way Monoj was listening to me , I realised ,standing by a person when he is emotionally charged and even feeling helpless, brings you very close to the person.

We had good match .We won by 68 runs .We could qualify for the second round only.

Cricket didn't give me much but teach some very valuable practical lessons in the company of some very good seniors. We respected them a lot .One such was N.K.Naryan. He was gold medallist in physics and was working as bank manager in the SBI. When we got late for the practice he often said, "You will not study more than me , yes you can't ,if you spend your time at square ,near girls' school, in some other rubbish activities, it is impossible. He further added , "Study at the time of study and play at the time of play, don't mix up. You will manage both well," We could not answer him back he always had points to convince. Other seniors like Amit Singh and Nehaluddin Ahamad had something which, we unknowingly tried to emulate.

Our next tour to Jamshedpur was even more exciting. It was U-19 tournament. We reached in the evening. We had our accommodation in the JRD Sports Complex, adjacent to Keenan Stadium. It was very hot and humid. After taking bath most of us came out to walk around the stadium .Some very young members of team were very excited to see the stadium where International matches were played. We were fascinated to see the sports environment of that place.

In those days Pakistan were playing against Sri.Lanka.I was out with Monoj and Amitesh. We were in front of the Keenan stadium. There was a small park .We sat at one corner of the park and were talking about the expected final eleven for the next day match. Just then Ratnesh came and said, "Pakistan lost the match,"

"It was expected as Pakistan's top order had collapsed in the beginning,"Amitesh said.

"Qamar you must be sad,"Ratnesh said smiling.

"Why should I be?" I said.

"No you people support Pakistan. You fire crackers when they win matches," He further said.

"You are mistaken dear. Because of some handful fools, don't blame the whole community. Even some time they do because of your kind of people," I said.

"Your kind of people , what do you mean? He said.

"I mean ,I know some of them. Since you put your words into their mouth, they do it to show you," I said, trying to make him understand.

Monoj and Amitesh were listening to us. They tried to stop us but I wanted to make my point clear to them.

"You know Ratnesh my grandfather was a freedom fighter. we all are proud of it.You can see his name, Syed Abdul Ghafoor, engraved on the rock installed in the courtyard of Zila School, to commemorate all the freedom fighters from that school. My father has been serving the people indifferent capacity, irrespective of their caste and religion. Love for our country in our gene. But we don't need certificate from anybody," I said in one go. Perhaps my tone was rather soft.

"Leave na yaar, concentrate on tomorrows' match," Monoj said .He sounded rather irritated.

"you know Ratnesh , it is very unfortunate that our patriotism is judged by the way few people react after watching a cricket a match. Pages of Indian history are filled with the stories of sacrifices, made by our fore-father. Monuments like Gateway of India, Victoria Memorial and many other still bear the names of all those people who selflessly gave their life for this country. And great many of them happen to be Muslim . If we have major Somnath Sharma on the one side, there is Abdul Hameed on the other. During 1962,war against China, Meer Usman Ali of Hydrabad, gave tons of gold to bail our country out of that financial crisis," I said. I wanted to speak more. In the mean time we started moving back to our rooms.

"We are blamed for supporting Pakistan. In fact we rejected the very idea of Pakistan. To be honest we Indian Muslim have suffered a lot because of Pakistan. They have not done any good to us and they can't do. They stand nowhere in front of our economy and cultural diversity. But still comparison is made. If at all we have to compare ourselves ,we ought to compare with some developed nation like France and Germany," I said.

"Is your speech over? Monoj said.

"Manager must be searching for us,"Amitesh said.

Fact remains that the world has suffered more because of the problem of co-existence, than any natural calamity. If we cut down our defence budget and the same is used in the education and health sector, the situation would be far better that what we have today.

We have always been culturally and religiously sensitive and this has often lead to conflict and sometime even riots. Political parties have off late started using this for polarising their votes. And the real issues are dusted under the carpet. Over the years this has dented the strong bond of unity of our country. Our strength and beauty lie in the cultural diversity. This colours the very fabrication of our society.

During my childhood our next door neighbour was an Agarwal family. Rupesh Kumar, alias Babloo was my close friend. We never had any sense of differences on the bases of religious practices. We and our family stood by each other whenever we had any problem. We were so close that when Agarwal uncle was getting her eldest daughter married , he searched for my father for her 'bidayee'. 'Chachi' was always there in case of any problem like a true neighbour. We were used to looking for each other at all important occasions of our family.

Much later, they, all of a sudden, sold their house and left our mohallah for good. We as children didn't understand the reason. After so many years I understood that that was the starting of the manifestation of the spreading of the intolerance based on the differences in religious and cultural beliefs. But majority of us still have the same feelings for all those who, keeping pace with the changed time, buzzed off. And I perceive, they too have same amount of emotional attachments with the time and incidences ,experienced with us.

My father loved talking about his friends. He had a host of exemplary friends. Ashok uncle, Ganesh uncle ,Mahendra uncle M.P. Singh uncle are few to name. One day I was sitting with my father. He was talking about his students who had done well in their life. In the meantime there was as an international call on my eldest brother's mobile. One uncle wanted to talk to my father. The caller was his son. My father being hard hearing, my brother put his phone on the speaker and gave to my father. We could see the happiness on the face of my father. He was

Rudra Pratap Singh uncle from the USA. He had breathing problem, hence he couldn't talk much. After talking to him we saw some tiny drop of tears, rolling down on the face of my father. His son said, "Dad is bed ridden now. He has been insisting upon making a call to India and make him talk to uncle (my father) for many days .He remembers him very fondly. He keeps talking about his college days and his friendship with uncle at Hazaribagh."

"It was so kind of you to make him talk to my father. He was very happy to have words with him. Thank you very much!" My brother said and he dropped the phone. We had witnessed how love, for friends, transcends all the boundaries of region and religion. My father looked very emotional after talking to Singh uncle.

Ours is a beautiful country in spite of all riots, brawl, scuffle on some silly issues, we often see people coming out of their houses to extend helping hands to the needy irrespective of their caste and religion. Cricket has been a good example of cultural diversity of the country. Cricketers from North, South, East and West set example of the vibrant colour of the culture they hold dear ,especially during celebration, and that turns out to be a melting pot of culture.

We had passion for cricket but comments and unwanted suggestions from the people around were undermining it. Most of us started making desperate attempt to catch the last straw. Some of them even made it .We needed some -body who would instil hope in us. The way hope sustains life in the same that would make us play for some more years with the same enthusiasm. Hope gives natural strength. As long as it thrives in you, circumstances can't defeat you. It is the same which makes us find out ways and prove 'where there is a will there is a way'. Hopelessness kills all the positivity in you. In case of disease it kills the immunity or defence mechanism of the body. It makes way for the disease to gnaw our body.

Once in the USA a culprit was given death sentence. A doctor planned to do an experiment. He took prior permission from the concerned authority. He went to that person a few days before the hanging.

He said, "Tomorrow you will be hung."

"Yes, I know." The culprit replied.

The doctor again said , "You see hanging is painful ,therefore we want you to die in less pain." He wanted to convince that culprit that his intention is to lessen the pain in his death.

That culprit smiled and said, "How?"

The doctor said, "Instead of hanging we will get you bitten by a cobra , what do you say?"

"In any way I have to die. There is no hope of life for me," The culprit said. "IT doesn't make any difference how my soul leaves my body." He further mentioned. He agreed with the doctor

On the scheduled date, with the permission letter the doctor with his assistants reached into the cell. They had one box in which they had put a black cobra. After all the formalities, one of them opened the box and showed the cobra, coiled inside the box, to the culprit. They put a thick black cloth on his eyes and was tied with a chair. His hands were cuffed. The doctor took out a pin , which had been joined at one end, to give the shape of snake teeth. He lifted his trouser and pierced .The pin made two marks. Small drops of blood came out from those marks. The doctor came out from the cell. After an hour they again went into the cell. They found the man lying dead on the chair .His body seemed poisoned.

The very experiment gave a new dimension to the line of thinking in the medical sciences. Now they could relate the effectiveness the medicine with the mental state of the patient. The culprit died because his pre-set negativity had killed all his immunity, consequently he succumbed to the very thought that he had been bitten by a poisonous snake and he would die. In addition to it he had lost all his 'will to live'.

Fact remains that most of us are bitten by the 'snake of negativity' day in and day out. Sometimes this is self-created. We allow others to disturb our balance of thoughts. Our expectations are directly proportional to the disappointments, we have in our life. It snatches our happiness. It leads to hopelessness , which is the pirate on the path of success. It loots our effort within a minute. There is a simple way to avoid this looting and that is –in the journey of success we should include those people who are deprived and helpless. Whatever the little we achieve we should share with others.

History is filled with the names which never let hopelessness, caused by comments and attitudes of the people around, finish their immunity. Rather they always looked at the light, found at the end of a tunnel. They had tunnel vision about their life.

Nelson Mandela was confined into an 8*8 room. He remained there for 26 long years. For a tall and lanky fellow, it was an impossible journey. He could do it by virtue of his tenacity, perseverance, resilience and never-say-die-attitude. The mentioned adjectives take birth in a person when they place their aim or goal of life above everything. For Mandela, 'Freedom' was the only charm which made him bear all that physical pain. The shackles and walls of the prison had to bow down before his 'iron-spirit'. He magnified his goal of 'freedom' of his people from the white authority, to such an extent that he had no time to see the magnitude of the challenges thrown on the way.

There are numerous of examples of people, in different fields, who by dint of their consistent effort and determination, achieved what they had dreamt of .For the consistency in the effort they had learnt how to 'keep on holding the ground or moderate themselves'. Once Sachin Tendulkar was asked who motivated him and how he remained motivated. He said, "I motivate myself." This self-motivation may be reasoned by various things such as –Extreme Love, anger, revenge , deep seated desire to prove ones worth etc.

Among all the mentioned reasons for the motivation which make a person put in tireless effort to achieve the set goal, Love has been the most powerful one. It makes persons detach from the time and space. I came across a few who dived into it.

When we used to play cricket, a girl often came to the ground with cake and chocolate for one of our team -mates, he happened to be a friend of mine. He got chance to talk to that girl, without getting disturbed, a little away from there, in lieu of those cakes and chocolates .He often cycled long distance in the evening , just to have a glimpse of hers. Hiding behind bushes for a chance to have words, ignoring all the danger which could have been there , needed a very power of love and passion from within. Loaning from friends to give costly greeting cards was quite common. Sometime bearing all those harsh words from people and even friends ,was the proof of his determinations and resilience.

One day I was getting back from the market. It must be 8:30.And those days it was late for any age group. I happened to meet a boy named Krish. He was quite young and energetic. He wished me first. I stopped for a while. I noticed he was carrying something. And he was going somewhere, in the opposite direction of his house. In fact that path lead to a big mango orchard, which was at the periphery of the mohallah. I was surprised.

"Krish what are you carrying and where are you going now ?" I said. He tried to hide, but failed.

"I am carrying this Odomos and bread." He said reluctantly.

"Odomos and bread !.I exclaimed.

"And where are you going dear?" I said.

He blushed and said, "I am going to meet her. Since her house is at the end, there are lots of mosquitoes and dogs. I have to talk through window from the orchard side. Before talking I apply odomos on the body and give bread to the barking dogs so that we might talk unintrupted."I was dumbstruck .I wished him luck and moved on .I could well realize the power of the emotion ,which made Dashrath Manjhi ,dug up the whole mountain to make way for his wife. I feel, had that love been directed toward any other goal they could have achieved that. It is all about effort in the right direction.

Big purpose (goal) fills us with enthusiasm .A.P.J.Abdul Kalam in his Wings of Fire , urges youth to dream big and not to lower their sight. According to him 'real dream is the one which we dream while waking up'. The journey from the present position to the position one desires in life, becomes easy ,if the purpose or goal of life is fixed. The moment we become aware of our goal or purpose of life , we start our journey of success. It doesn't matter much where do we stand, what matters the most is the direction we stand at. Even if we have the best of conveyance like Mercedez, ferari, etc , but without right direction we never reach our destination.

Yes, our purpose or goal of life should be based on reality. This will vary person to person. Only desires and imagination can't be called goal or purpose. It has to be the result of proper self-exploration. Once the goal matches with our interest and later passion ,the same makes us have single –minded devotion for it.

Hungarian shooter , Karoly Takacs , is a classic example of self-motivation and single-minded devotion. He was in the Hungarian Army. In 1936 , he was world class pistol shooter. But he was denied a place in the Hungarian Shooting team for the 1936 Summer Olympics because he was a Sergeant and only Commissioned officers were given place in the team , to compete in the prestigious international arena. The restriction was lofted in Hungary , after the Berlin games. He was expected to win a gold in 1940 Summer Olympics, scheduled to be held in Tokyo. But the fate had a different story, prepared for him.

During an army training in 1938 , his 'right and shooting hand' was badly injured when a faulty grenade exploded near his hand. Now he could not do shooting with that hand. The sporting world shelved his name .His was only an end-story for the world. Though hugely disappointed in the beginning he, after few months , was all set to hit the shooting arena with extra ounce of courage and determination. He started his practice with his only hand. He did not let the world know. He practiced at a secret place , away from the sight of the media and people related to sports. Within a year he surprised his countrymen by winning national championship. Now he was in Hungarian

National team. But his fate was to test him again. The Olympics games scheduled for 1940 and 1944 were cancelled due to the second World War. Takacs didn't cancel his practice. He did more than usual time. He took the world by surprise when he won gold medal in the Summer Olympics at the age of 38.He beat the Olympics favourite Argentine Carlos Diaz, who was the then world champion. Carlos Diaz had approached him before the event and asked what he was doing there, as he had heard and read about his accident . Karoly replied that he was there to learn how to set world record. Diaz, later, congratulated him, saying, 'you have learnt enough'.

Giving example of big personalities may not be a good idea for the people , as most of them don't become example. But getting ideas, based on the personal experience of the successful people, reflected through their story, have worked for many. Rain drops fall equally everywhere but the results are different. If they fall into a tank, they become part of it. Some drops fall into the sea , they become sea. When some drops fall on the barren land, they lose their existence for good. Some lucky drops fall on the fertile ground and they become reason for the happiness of the farmers. The same drop falls into the mouth of a snake, it becomes poison and if the same falls into a sheep, it becomes pearl. The rain is same but the result varies to the extent that at one place it gives life while on the other it takes life .All depend on the environment the rain drops get.

To achieve greatness, only having great desire in not enough. The intensity of the same ought to make the person ignore all those things which come on his way. It frees them from time and space. It doesn't allow them to get tired. Michael Angelo often forgot time during his work.

We had no one around who would make us feel the importance of positive thinking. We had the desire but that never became the propelling factor. We continued to play with lots of uncertainties and doubts in us. In such state of mind we once again went to Jamshedpur to paly U-19tournament.We were quite used to of the scorching of the steel city. It was test of resilience and mental toughness of the people who were out either for duty or some works. Roads and public places bore deserted look. Our match ended at around 11-11:30AM.We won our first match against Plamu, comprehensively. I scored fifty and Monoj bowled well with 3/21.We won the second match against Dumka and qualified for the quarter final. We were to play against star- studded Jamshedpur in the quarter final. Some of us were quite excited and desperate to play against Jamshedpur as we wanted to put up a good show. We had our team meeting in the evening itself. Some very common points were discussed. After the meeting our team manager Mr.C.P.Singh said to our captain , "Go and get tickets reserved for Hazaribagh otherwise it will be difficult tomorrow."

"Why tickets today? We have match tomorrow."I said quizzically.

"Do you think you will defeat Jamshedpur? There are five Ranji players in the team." He said emphatically.

"So what? We can defeat them. We are playing good cricket."Monoj Said.

"I know what you all will do." The manager said smilingly. It hurt us .It demoralized us. We were helpless. Our manager was asking us to accept defeat without playing. In fact most of us had lost hope. Only formalities were to be observed next day.

"Captain, do as I say." He said in an authoritative tone.

Next day we reached the ground beforehand. Jamshedpur players started arriving one by one on bike and cars. They were looking impressive with their costly Kit bags ,goggles, headphones etc. We were fascinated towards them. This fascination had an element of subjugation. Any way the match started. Some very senior officials of BCA(Bihar Cricket Association) were there to watch the match. We restricted Jamshedpur at 181in 35 overs. Since the Loyla Ground was small therefore the target was gettable.

Hazaribagh were 26 for four. I was there at one end. Rajesh came to bat .We both started taking singles , twos and boundaries in between. Just then Rajesh ,while playing a Yorker got a ball on his right toe. The nail came out and it was bleeding profusely. The whole stand was quite. Rajesh got out after scoring his fifty. Hazaribagh were 126 for five now. Players from other districts were also there to cheer for us. I got out at 66.Hazaribagh needed twenty odd runs to win. Our captain brought himself down in the order out of nervousness and we collapsed at 171.After the match some of officials came to meet me. They patted and appreciated me for my batting. Rajesh also got lots of appreciations. On that day it was all the more clear to me that every day is a new day and it is performance, on the ground ,on that day, matters , not the name ,label or past records.

Finally we had lost the match as expected and planned by our manager. Next morning we were at Bus stand to board bus for Hazaribagh. Monoj came with the newspaper. There was big news about our performance. My name was quite prominent in that. Reading the newspaper ,Monoj said to me , "This time your selection is sure."

"Let's see, what happens." I said.

I came back home. My father was happy as he someone had told him about our match especially about my performance. Now everyday I read newspaper particularly to get the news about the scheduled U-19 state camp. Days kept rolling down. One day after getting back from the morning practice I was casually turning the pages of the newspaper. I was disheartened to read 'Bihar U-19 team fly for Guwhati'.I had so many questions in my mind. Why? Didn't I deserve to be in the camp at least? Was my performance not good enough? and so on. I wept a lot telling my father about this. My father consoled me saying , "Have patience Beta! Something better is waiting for you.

Later my cousin went to Jamshedpur to play U-15.He was asked about me by one of the officials, about my not joining U-19 state camp .He said that the letter had been sent to HDCA(Hazaribagh District Cricket Association). Monoj wanted me to make enquiry, but it was no use crying over spilt milk. Later I was told by a reliable source that the 'call letter' had come but misplaced in the office. I had nothing to do except to see my fate turning away from me. This was a blow to my aspiration. This happens to so many cricketers even now. They are informed late knowingly or unknowingly.

'The fire in (my) the belly'(this happens to be the title of a book written by Narita,my student) was counting its day. Now I had eyes all around as if they were asking 'how long? In the meantime I was informed that I had been picked up for the senior district tournament , to be held at Bokaro Steel City. My family quite reluctantly gave me the permission, as it was the month of Ramzan. We won couple of matches comfortably. I scored fifty in one match. My team-mates helped me a lot in playing while fasting. I used to do bat only. Twelfth man used to do fielding for me. In the night I was woken up by Monoj for my early morning meal , 'sehar'.That was an emotional moment for me.I was proud of my teammates who were the true souls of our cultural diversity.

We had our last match against the host team, Bokaro Steel City. It was at Training Hostel ground. The ground was packed with local audience. But the weather had different mood. Dark clouds were scudding over us. Heavy rain was expected at any point of time. This match was to decide which team would make it to the 'A' division. We batted first and were booked at 116.It was an easy chase for the host team. To win the match on the average basis , the host team was to play at least fifteen overs. Our lunch time was cut short. The officials ,from Jamshedpur were putting pressure on us to get ready as fast as possible so that the second inning might be started early .They seemed hell bent on giving match in their favour. The game started. The host team, seeing the weather condition, started hitting the ball to the fences. I was in the audience. I could see the happiness of the people. They had two options one-to chase the target given or play at least 15 overs without losing many wickets. But as soon as the third ball of the fourteen over bowled, it started raining heavily . We were happy as we wanted to play re-match. We got back to our dressing room. It kept raining for two hours. The whole ground including the mating-wicket was complete under water. We were shocked to see the locals in the ground. They were with sack, saw dust, bucket and other things to sponge out the water from the ground. After half an hour couple of volunteers came and asked our captain to get ready for the game.

"Game now? The wicket is wet. We cannot play in this condition." Our captain said.

The volunteers went back. We had changed our uniform. After few minutes one of the umpires came and asked us to come to the ground in ten minutes. "But sir, wet mat can't be used unless it dries up completely, according to the rules!" Our captain put forward the same argument, but he was not interested in listening. My team had to get ready.

I had batted, and in the first inning, twelfth man was doing the fielding. The team had decided to delay as much as possible by bowling wide ball, no ball and other kind of invalid balls. The host team needed only eight ball to be bowled for winning the match in run rate. It took 30 minutes to bowl eight balls. The wicket keeper had removed his pad and was standing at boundary. I could feel the restlessness of the audience. They were getting irritated. They wanted their home team to win and qualify for the next level. For the first time I saw a cricket match was being played by eleven plus several hundred audience. They were so much involved in the match that they should have been called 'non-playing players'. The moment fifteenth over got over the whole audience was in the ground .They started beating our players like any thing ,especially our captain and wicket keeper. Players were chased and thrashed wherever they went . One player wanted to hide himself in a quarter nearby. The owner pushed him out saying , "We have young girls in our family."

After the whole 'hungama' we were in the dressing room. We were scared .Police had come .We were escorted to the bus stand to board bus for Hazaribagh. But we got seats in a mini bus. On the way near Ramgarh, our wicketkeeper spotted a boy in the bus, who was there among the active audience, who had beaten us. Our players stated beating that boy on the bus itself. The bus was stopped on the way. There were hardly four other passengers on the bus. They couldn't dare stop us. That boy was beaten black and blue and sent back to Bokaro , with swollen face and bleeding mouth. This was a kind of consolation for our players, who had experienced, one of the most bizarre happenings in the game of cricket.

Now ,after quite a few years of those cricketing years, when I do introspection about my failure in achieving successful height ,I find it is my fear of getting out which had taken a huge toll of my talent. I could never play fearlessly. This fear was not of getting hit by the ball but about failing to score runs. This often restricted me from playing shots, which could have given me more runs , consequently selection for higher level.

Fear is the biggest obstacle on the path of success. Fear hides the destination. Every individual suffers from fear psychosis of one thing or other. There are people who have more artificial fear than the real ones. This fear finishes our self-respect. Many time we have to surrender our will before this fear. If this fear is not removed at the right time , it can destroy our talent.

Some people have self –created fear .These people are scared of everything like-every individual wants to cheat him, every disease can take his life. According to the expert, 98% of our fear is meaningless. Only 2% happens and that too doesn't harm us. We can conquer the world if we conquer our fear. According to research, there are six kinds of fear which pull us back from the path of success ; (i.) Fear of disease (ii). Fear of getting poor (iii). Fear of death (iv). Fear of criticism (v.) Fear of losing prestige.(vi). Fear of fear of losing love (vii). Fear of getting old etc.

Some of the fears are inevitable. They are the part of natural growing up. Shying away from those fears makes it very difficult for us to accept them as usual happenings. The more we take time to accept, the more we are frightened. In case of a disease, when a person is diagnosed with Diabetes, they take time to accept it .As a result their health starts running down. But when they adjust with medication and other routine activities , they again become normal. Roosvelt had said , "All we have to fear is fear itself."

Mat Haig in his book 'Reason to Stay Alive', writes, "The world is increasingly designed to depress us. Happiness isn't very good for the economy. If we were happy with what we had, why would we need more? How do you sell an anti-ageing moisturiser ? You make somebody worry about ageing. How do you get people to vote for a political party? You make them worry about immigration .How do you get them to buy insurance ? By making them worry about everything. How do you get them to have plastic surgery ? By highlighting their physical flaws. How do you get them to watch a TV-show? By making them worry about missing out. How do you get them to buy a new smartphone ? By making them feel like they are being left behind."[1]

Fact remains that, to overcome all the fear, created with the vested interest, we need to have lots of control over our emotions. And this level control is only possible when we have unshakeable belief on the Almighty. We need to have balance of reasons, based on logic, scientific and social theories ,practicality of life and religious beliefs. In our life most of the happenings are unprecedented .And we can't do anything .We have to accept them and move ahead.

(1.Reason to Stay Alive-Mat Haig-chapter, The World ,page 189.)

It was January and Hazaribagh was experiencing biting cold. Cold wave was forcing people to be in .For warm water we used immersion rod. My kit bag was lying on the middle shelf ,along with some clothes .My CA bat, which my father had got for me from Pakistan by an uncle whose son lived there .There was a switch board next to the shelves. An immersion rod was in bucket, on the floor. It was cold morning therefore most members were still on their bed. I happened to be in the room and I was horrified to see fire on the shelf. Thank God I didn't go straight to the shelf but I rushed towards the main switch. I didn't have time to call people. I managed to pull the lever of the switch and got back to the room. I found the immersion rod was, lying on the shelf which was still red and its plug was still on. Other switches next to it had been put off. My kit bag with clothes had been completely burnt. Luckily the fire didn't reach to the bat. In the meantime other members of the family had reached. My younger sister was weeping at one corner of the room. She was frightened. She told that she had made that mistake. In hurry she lifted the rod and placed on the shelf after switching off the wrong switch. My father looked at me and smiled. He said, "Son! Never mind there must be something good hidden in it." But I thought that it was a kind of hint, being dropped by Almighty to call it a day for cricket.

CHAPTER FIVE

New Awakening

I had graduated from St. Columba's college. Now! What next? Was an important question. My father had one straight line.

He said , "Continue your study!"

I said , "Yes!,

"Go, take admission in M.A! My father said emphatically. I couldn't say no.

I took admission although I had no clear picture what I was going to do. Now I am reminded , what Bob Proctor had said, "Everything that is coming into your life you are attracting into your life. And it is attracted to you by the virtue of the images you are holding in your mind ,"

Law of attraction is common for the students. Especially those who study Physics. The same works in our life also but very few of us realise. Rohnda Byrne in his book 'The Secret' says , "You are the most powerful magnet in the universe. You contain a magnetic power within you that is more powerful than anything in the world and this unfathomable magnetic power is melted through your thoughts."

Our situations are the result of our own thoughts. What we think we become. Most of the people want to change their life but they don't change their thoughts. Our situations are not our selection but we can certainly select our thoughts. The result of the situations depends upon our approach towards the situations. That may be problem oriented i.e we tend to concentrate on the problem not the solution the other one is solution oriented which pushes us towards the finding of the solutions. If we want to improve our performance, our thoughts should converge on one point around the solution. We should talk to those people who have conditioned themselves to have solution oriented approach. Talking to those people fills you with optimism.

Every thought is like a seed and our mind is a garden. If good plants are planted, unwanted weeds come up, which need to be weeded out. Those weeds get roots when we talk to people with negative attitude. This negativity holds back the positivity in us. Since our thoughts are the threshold force which triggers off our actions, they need to be kept from negativity.

One thought begets one action .If we do that action repeatedly that becomes our habit and when our habit becomes rooted that shapes our character and our character makes our fate. Therefore to change destiny we have to change our thoughts. Good thoughts produce good attitude and our attitude decides our altitude. Our present situation is the result of the thoughts in the past. It never happens that if we think good but we don't get good result. Sometime the result apparently may not be according to our wish but in the long run we get good harvest of those good thoughts. A student should not think about failure they should think about achieving rank. It is not all about thinking once but consistency is needed in our thinking. We will have to think about our goal and success again and again.

The origin of human action is 'thought' .The validity of an action depends on the validity of thoughts. Many a times it happens that the more we try to avoid a thing, the more it comes on our way. Therefore one negative idea attracts negative result. It seems that what manifests from our thought, doesn't take 'NOT' from our idea. I didn't want to be in the teaching line .Because I saw my father teach since I had opened my eyes. He had to struggle in most part of his life. My mother was never in favor of any of our brothers, joining teaching profession. The very idea must be in our thoughts and with the passage of time I as well as my two brothers was catapulted in the teaching profession. Visualizing one's goal or getting one with the target ,opens avenues to achieve it. But to be in this position one must have a specific goal. During 1980's and early 90's one could see antenna on almost every second roof. We used to adjust it according to the signal. In our career also , keeping our thoughts in the specific direction is a must. The positive or negative thoughts work as a magnetism. They pull the things according to their intensity. It develops tilt and the very tilt decides the attraction .This ultimately turns out to be guiding factors for the actions we engage ourselves with. An overall image of a person is the sum total of his actions and sayings and these two are the manifestations of our thoughts.

Jack Canfield says, "Decide what you want .Believe you can have it. Believe you deserve it and believe it's possible for you. Then close your eyes every day for several minutes and visualize having what you already want."

In our case, most of us didn't have very clear idea about our goal .We were like dried leaves floating on the water. This happens when our priorities are not well defined. Hence our actions don't match with something very specific and well planned. It also leads to a situation wherein things are not systematic. We suffer from 'dependence syndrome'. We depend on people, time, and opportunity. Ours was the time, career counseling was not heard of. Suggestions from parents and elders were the ultimate resources available to us. We even lacked self-awareness. We neither had idea about our passion or X factors or any specific ability. Yes, we knew how to play all sorts of games. Now, thank God, it is given due place in the education system. CBSE, has, off late , accommodated it in its year planner.

In those days trend of quizzing started. The topics covered, were from the general syllabus of competitive exams. Few had cracked exams. We too developed interest in quizzing but still the goal was not well defined. Therefore we lacked planning. But by now we had understood that life wanted us to do something, called 'making career'.

I had taken admission in M.A . Although , I was not interested. My father had made up his mind to make me do masters. Class started. I was sincerely attending classes .We had a good circle which included some of the most talented girls I have ever come across. We were god friends, defying the normal social belief. The society has never had room enough to accept a healthy friendship between a boy and a girl. I understood it, hence I created and environment wherein they had direct access to my home and family members .I deliberately made them introduce with my mother ,sisters and sister-in-law. I did it to remove all the room for others to murmur or fabricate story out of that. During those days I had a friend , Narendra. He was interested in of our classmates. She was close to me. I often visited her house. Uncle and aunty were noble souls. One day I went to her hour house to discuss about a programme , scheduled on one of the coming days ,in our department. She was our ace singer. Any cultural programe could not have been thought of without her. I went to Narendra first .While talking I informed her about my plan. He had prepared his meal. He forced me to eat. We had rice and 'sabji' on the same plate. Neither of us had any inhibition in doing so. Religion never came on our way.

I reached her home. After twenty minutes Narendra was there .Seeing him she wished him , "Good afternoon bhaiya!" "Good afternoon ,"Narendra replied in rather dull done. I could sense his discomfort with the way he replied. We were talking about programme and all of a sudden Narendra said , "Wht is your plan for marriage?"

"I will let you know when I get married , bhaiya," She answered. This was a final blow to Narendra's flickering hope.

Ours was a good batch during masters. One day a friend of ours expressed his desire to celebrate his birth day in the department .Actually he was interested in one girl.He wanted to have an opportunity to spend some time with her and all of us.Couple of friends knew this. We decided to go to our H.O.D and seek permission.

"Sir, Rajesh wants to celebrate his birth day,"I said

"Why are you asking me ?"Sir Said quizzically.

"Actually sir,he wants to celebrate in the department itself and invite all our sirs,"Bhaskar said clarifying to sir.

"What ? In the department !He exclaimed.

He thought for some time and said, "OK! But next time don't come for the permission to celebrate some rituals here ,"He gave consent saying.

" No sir,we will not come,"We said.

Few classmates including those two , were very active .They planned to get the shopping for the celebration done by the same girl, Rajesh was interested in. We, therefore convinced her to accompany us to the market . we asked her choose a shirt , tie and a perfume. We got all the item in the same market. When she left those two wrote 'Presented to Rajesh by .....the name of the girl. They got the gift wrapped with beautiful paper. That girl had absolutely no idea whatsoever about it.

Next day we celebrated the birth day. Pack of snacks was distributed among the teachers and classmates. We sang birthday song .Rajesh also sang song but before that he thanked teachers and all of us for making his days. Finally the gift was presented to him by our head of the department. Rajesh looked ecstatic. When the teachers and the girls were gone we asked Rajesh to open the gift. We were excited for the moment when he would read the written name and message at the back of the pack. One of those two cunningly got that part of the pack exposed as to make him read the name.

He said , "Rajesh read the message,"

Rajesh took the pack and read the written lines with name. He was blushing. That gave us unwonted joy. From the next day Pooja vacation started we didn't meet to get the feedback. After the vacation we were in the class, waiting for the teacher to come. We had forgotten about the B'day celebration. During pooja only our date sheet for the exam had been announced. We, therefore ,wanted to concentrate on our study. We were talking about the syllabus and other examination related things. Just then that girl appeared from behind and started shouting at us. "What do you understand yourself? I know everything what you people did to that fellow," She said.

"I will tell sir everything what you did. How dare you play with somebody's reputation and emotion! She added angrily.

"What would we do, he was interested in you .We wanted to help him," Vipul said.

"What ? He is interested in me !Is he ok ?She said, calming down herself.

We made her and her friends sit and convinced her .Thank God Rajesh didn't come on that day. And the story which could have been ended with ugly scene, ended , leaving Rajesh guessing for some time ,the possible reaction from her.

This happens in most of the cases. It remains one sided and fizzles out .We met Rajesh during our final year exam but didn't have time to discuss anything other than preparation and topics covered.

CHAPTER SIX

AN EPOCH MAKING

After the exam, one day Narendra came and told that one of our classmates was getting married at Ranchi and we had been invited. Some of us planned to attend the marriage. I, Narendra and few more attended the marriage party and while returning Narendra asked me to accompany him to Ghatotand, where he had joined a school. I had heard a lot of Ghatotand from my cousins, as their brother-in-laws had lived at this place for years. I had heard about live performance of big artists including Jagjit Singh and about very good atmosphere of sports. Somewhere in the corner of my heart there was a little desire to visit this place. I got ready with a condition that I would return Hazaribagh the very next day. It was a small but beautiful township, settled in the midst of mines and dump-yards. Tata Steel gets its coal, mined here. We reached in the evening. After some time Narendra introduced me with some of his colleagues.

"Meet Qamar, he is joining our school,"Narendra said. I had no idea. I had not even thought of it. I smiled but I didn't say anything. When we got to our room I said , "What is this Narendra, you didn't tell me about this .I am not interested in joining school now.

"Nothing will happen, just appear in the interview. I will not ask you to join,"Narendra said. "I am doing it, as I was asked to bring a teacher of English language and literature ,"He further added.

Next day he took me his school. I was relaxed as there was no pressure of job interview. Because I didn't intend to join teaching as profession. This disinterestedness towards teaching profession because the atmosphere I was brought up in I had seen my father giving tuition in the very cold early morning, sitting on the mat .A rough 'chadar' used to be there on his shoulder. My mother didn't want me to be a teacher. Neither of us demeaned teaching profession but the way my father had gone through the tough time, being a teacher, was the reason for the repulsion. My father didn't get salary on the regular basis. He made every possible effort to meet the expenses of the family. Nevertheless we were very happy with whatever the little we had. We didn't mind wearing trousers with some patches on its back. This was normal. Many of my friends used to wear.

We are rich or poor depends on our thoughts. Our outer world is the reflection of our inner world. We are rich if we compare ourselves with person below our level and we are poor if we compare ourselves with the persons above our level. It proves that 'comparison' with others makes us rich or poor. In fact the biggest poverty is that we consider ourselves needy and poor. Ours was the time when comparison was not in vogue. Therefore contentment had a prominent place in our approach.

Is our past, present or future in our control? **Past came to teach us that we should remember the results of our past experiments , actions and experiences and move ahead.** We can't bring about any change in the result of the past by applying any power of the world. Many people remain lost in the dream of the future. Although future doesn't have any reality. **Today is the true asset.** The best way to shape future is to live in present , using the resources available in the best possible way. Every moment , every day, every year is bidding adieu. We don't realize this, since we r always in the rat race. It is not important how many moments you lived, what is important ,how many moments we filled life in. True wisdom should enable us to not to lament about the past ,not to worry about the future but to polish our present.

Sometime our carelessness turns out to be a gift. When we are careless about our past , to the extent that we don't lose sight of the mistakes and the consequence ,faced thereby. Because people who learn from their failures know the reason of the failure and later succeed in their effort to achieve something in their life. The additional advantage with these people is they have the ability to maintain low profile and their head remains on their shoulder. And not worrying about future, so to say creating no self-mounted pressure in planning future. Doctors say 'avoid hurry worry and curry. Today, **worry for the future destroys our happiness of the present.** It doesn't allow us to celebrate the beautiful moment available with us in the present. We procrastinate , citing the example of future target or goal. In such a situation our happiness is 'iffy'(If this thing happens or that thing happens then we will celebrate).Thus that moment of real celebration never comes or we keep pushing them away.

It is good to be contented with whatever we have, but it is not at all good to be contented with whatever we are. Living in the present and polishing ourselves is the best way out to escape from being hijacked by past-thought or future-worries.

I was interviewed .It was not that impressive, I assume. Next I was asked to write an article on 'the general election'. It was, perhaps a written test. For the demonstration class Ms.Sheril , the senior most teacher, made me understand about the chapter, to be taught in class IX.I was to spend ten minutes in introduction ,ten minutes in telling the theme of the chapter and rest of the time I was to clear the doubts of the students. I finished everything in 15minutes .I didn't invite questions instead I started firing questions on the students. I was confident as I was not thinking about the outcome of the effort. I was least bothered about my selection. Now I understand the psyche which works in such situation. When we think too much about the result or outcome of our efforts, we become extra cautious, (more than required) and make mistakes. It happens with most of us. When we spend our good time thinking about the end, we fail to do justice with the means. If we concentrate just on means, the end has to be good.

For me it was a different experience altogether. I, coming from Hindi medium background, had always been fascinated by Convent schools .During my schooling, I, like all other Hindi medium students , had a complex. This complex was not based on the knowledge which the students of English medium schools had but their ability to communicate in English made us feel inferior. And when it came to girls' speaking in English, things became all the more fascinating. We failed to realize that speaking a language is just a skill .A person can learn any language at any point of time if they have will to learn. It doesn't have to do anything with the ability and creativity of the people.

We grew up in an environment in which speaking English language was considered as one of the most sought after qualities in students. That was also the qualification of being smart or fit enough to be befriended by girls ,studying in English medium Schools.

Knowingly or unknowingly the very bug of English Language had bitten me with great intensity. I got thrilled when my elder brothers talked to somebody in English. I used to listen to them secretly. We had formed a group of like-minded friends .We would sit near 'chhatt Talab' and do discussion in whatever the little we could do. Like all other beginners , each day I planned to speak couple of new sentences ,which I came across in the newspaper or book. When I succeeded in speaking in front of my friends as per my home-work, it gave me unwonted joy. Every single time it added an extra ounce of confidence in me. For me speaking in front of X'averian friends was a challenge. I kept trying for years but I couldn't do the way I wanted. There is a situation 'how to start' closes the door of how to start. Yes, I would speak few words and phrases in between , while talking to them.

Now I was getting offer to teach in an English medium school. I accepted and started going to school.I was putting up with Narendra. He used to prepare meal .I didn't know anything about cooking. I used to help in cleaning utensils. On the fourth day a neighbor ,Laxmi, came to me and said , "You have become popular sir,".

"How?" I said.

"Students are talking highly about you," He added. Narendra was also there .He reacted , saying , "This happens with every new Teacher."

After completing the probationary period of six days,I was paid Rs.106 per day.I told Narendra.

"How come you got Rs 106, I was given Rs. 76 only. I will ask the principal,"Narendra said.

Days rolled down I kept engaging the classes sincerely. Perhaps I was enjoying the reactions and response I was getting from the students. It was second month of my joining. Now Narendra didn't ask me for company when he went out in the evening. He used to go out to meet his acquaintances .One day he came in the evening and said, "Qamar , you leave school otherwise your parents will hold me responsible for trapping you here."

"How can I do this all of a sudden?" I replied.

"Why not? Go to the principal and say that your parents are not allowing you to continue." He said.

"I have some commitment with the school. I can't leave on the spur of the moment. I will have to inform the principal before-hand ." I said.

"Do you accept that I have brought you here? He said.

"Yes ,I do accept that you are the reason of my being here." I said.

"Then, I say , do whatever, but you leave. He said insisting.

I had no idea why he started behaving like that. Living with his imposed obligation, from his gesture, was difficult for me cope up with. After couple of days I had fever. I was lying on the cot in the same room where Narendra had his bed. He would come without noticing me. Couple of students came to meet me. They would often come. To my utter surprise he scolded them for wasting their time. I don't know whether it was his insecurity or any other thing which made him do this. Somehow I got well and decided to leave the school .Next day I decided to inform the principal about my leaving . I went to the principal and said, "Sister, I can't continue here now."

"Why? What happened?" Sister said.

"As long as I am in the school I am comfortable but outside the school campus I feel suffocated." I said.

"If place is the problem then we can give you accommodation near convent." Sister said.

"No sister I will not continue. Moreover my result is out and I have to go to Delhi for preparing myself for Civil Services." I said.

I left the school .This came as a surprise for many in the school. While coming out from the school gate I had not dreamt that my fate would drag me to this place again.

CHAPTER SEVEN

THROWING THE DICE

Now we had our masters in our hands. What next was still occupying our mind? Some of us, including me, hand to go to Delhi to prepare for the Civil Services. No one was there guide us . We were moving recklessly. without any strategy for the preparation.

Talent and ability are not the only ingredients , required to succeed I achieving the set goal. Bread and butter is not the issue. Almighty feeds the smallest of creatures which are at the bottom of the sea. Whosoever has taken birth gets food and they can't die until they have consumed the food, destined for them. But the big question is , HOW?

Purusuhttam Express goes to Delhi from the Koderma Station at 12:05.It has many coaches .AC ones, sleepers and general coaches. All these three different categories of coaches are filled with passengers. In the AC coaches , attendants keep coming at regular interval for the cleaning and for the other needs of the passenger. Passengers are provided with pillows, blankets and bed sheets etc. Breakfast and water bottle are complimentary .In the sleeper class one has freedom to stretch one's body and sleep and in the general class, coaches are manned in such a way that people don't have space to walk comfortably. Newspapers are spread on the floor for sleeping purposes .Passengers don't spare the space even between the two toilets.

Purushuttam Express reaches Delhi with all its passengers. It doesn't leave its general coach on the way and reach its destination. Similarly life passes .People grow old and die but the question, how one leads one's life needs to be contemplated. Like the ones in the AC class, passenger class or the general class. We need to be contented with whatever has been given by God but it certainly doesn't stop us from making effort to get luxuries of life through right means.

Complacency is the best or perhaps the only options left for us when it comes to complexion, height , feature etc. which we don't have any control on. Rest all the things we get through hard work, like being good in studies, good in any skill, needed in any field whether it's sports ,art, or any soft skill. To get these we have to come out from our 'comfort- zone' ,created with lots of love and affection by our parents and near and dear ones. Bearing the hardship of weather and remaining fixed on the set goal , and going through all the ups and downs on the path, make us 'mentally strong' or else we prove to be vulnerable to any change ,in place ,people or circumstance. Failing to cope up with the said change makes us 'strongly mental'

Here nature teaches us a lesson .Butterfly can't be a beautiful, which is admired and appreciated by onlookers , unless the larvae come out of their comfortable cocoon.

Small towns have a typical problem. People find themselves very attached to everything of the town. As a result they can't leave their town comfortably. This was all the more apparent and strong in our time. Even if they left they missed their adda and chowk. One of my acquaintances was going through monetary crisis. He got a job in other state. He was to stay and work there. He was a father of two sons. He was found weeping on phone in first two or three days. And after 13 days he left the job and got back .He got back to be at his chowk and adda. This has been the problem of many people who, otherwise ,were very talented and could have done something big but they could not overcome their nostalgia.

After making a very weak plan we managed to come out from the strands of nostalgia. I had hope, riddled with so many ifs and buts. With this we headed towards Delhi.

We used to pass remark on those who had been to Delhi for the preparation but they couldn't make it. After reaching Delhi, I realized the saying 'only wearer knows where the shoe pinches' .Preparation for the civil services needed single minded devotion, which I was not able to give. In my sub-conscious mind there were many questions which needed answer. I was not able to give direction to my mind. And as long as one doesn't have crystal clear idea and direction about his goal one can't bridle one's mind. After this only, one has a tunnel vision of his goal. In this state one doesn't see anything other than his goal, like thing at the end of a tunnel.

The world offers us opportunities. At one time one gets only one. And to have it, one has to be one with it. To reach this state one has to convince oneself about that specific goal. Next is developing bond with it .We start loving everything associated with it. We visualize our goal. We sometime identify our-self with all those whom we idealize or emulate. In such a state we remain indifferent to external stimuli.

Newton's law can be applied in life as well. To move, everything needs threshold energy. To turn any movement into fruitful, we need ignition in the shape of counseling , motivational words ,may be a story or appreciation.

In the beginning of my cricket career I got a little support from my elder especially from Raju bhai. He supported me a lot. And in the Later stage when my confidence had been shattered and I needed somebody who would instil in me the must needed positivity to sustain , my father was there with little idea of career making avenues.

After reaching Delhi ,once again I found myself in the same state of mind. Seeing the environment of Mukherjee Nagar and all the civil services aspirants ,I was not able to muster up courage to take the situation head on. We stayed in Gandhi Vihar, a then newly developed residential area. As accommodation was not that costly there. I received Rs 1200 from my father. I could well understand how he must be sending that money. He had been stretching his income to the end to meet all the expenses .But for me that was not enough. I paid the whole twelve hundred for the rent. That was my share in the total rent, paid for the flat, shared with other friends. To meet other expenses like mess and study materials I started giving tuition. I used to go to Shaktinagar and by the time I returned it was around 8:30 or sometime 9:00 PM.I found myself drained out .Waking up late at night was proving to be difficult. But it was not impossible.

I could not do because I had not yet visualized my goal. I needed mental rehearsal about my goal and purpose of visiting Delhi. Nothing was clear in my mind. Things were jumbled in my mind.

Each day was teaching me a lesson. I could well understand how much effort was required for square of meals. I didn't eat pear-guard at home. Now I ate with relish .At the end of the month, moving with my friends and getting attracted towards a Tshirt and finding ways not to buy it. Then on Sunday ,Chor bazar' was the destination for us. Like me, so many used to gather there to buy things of their need. Although they were immaterial for anything big to be achieved in life. But these experiences were peeling off the layers of life. I would see tired office people, dozing off at the bus stop, while waiting for their bus. The screeching of the DTC busses would wake them up every now and then. I could see humans getting grinded in the 'grinding machine' called 'LIFE'

CHAPTER EIGHT

HOME CALLING

November 2000 came and after lots of political drama, the struggle for the separate Jharkhand state was to bear fruit. On 15th November 2020, Jharkhand got separated from Bihar. We were happy and excited, thinking about the possibilities of new job opportunities in our own sate.I got a letter from my father .He had asked me to return Hazaribagh. He wanted me to stay at home and prepare for other competitive examinations .He too expected new vacancies in the newly born state. But things didn't happen the way most of the people of Jharkhand had dreamt.

Finally I got back to Hazaribagh . But still no specific direction to go and work hard. How wonderful it was ? Months after months were rolling down in filling up forms and making half-hearted attempt. There was pressure on each one of us.

Strugglers have to face questions at every corner. We were not exceptions. What are you doing? Why did you get back from Delhi? Why don't you fill this or that form? and so on. We tried to answer in yes or no. It was indeed annoying for us at that point of time. As, now we understand that those questions carried care, concern and worry of those good people of the society.

Actually society knowingly or unknowingly does a favour by making queries to the young ones especially those, who are on the verge of taking responsibilities of the society. It happens and it has always happened in at least all the middle class society. Sometime those questions make us reflect on our ways. And we were mindlessly spending our time .We were scattered in our approach. We were demotivated not because opportunities were not there but we had narrowed our vision. What added salt to injury was the inability to take initiative. For that, our mind had become numb. Time was slipping out of our hand like the hour glass. We were desperate to do something. In such a situation one day I met a friend of mine. We played lots of cricket together. He told me that he was doing business of cable wire. He had some ligament issue in his knees. As I too had developed the same therefore we often talked about precaution and exercises needed to put check to the pain. I casually asked him where he was going.

He said, " Gahtotand".A customer owes me money there."

The word Ghatotand rang a bell in the mind. It resurfaced all the good memories ,associated with the place. Suddenly I developed a strong urge to visit that place. I don't know whether that was a genetic call for the teaching profession to which my father belonged and I had grown up watching his passion for the same.

"Oh! How will you go there ?" I said inquisitively.

"On bike". He replied.

I felt as if I was being pulled by an unknown force. Instantly I decided to go there.

"If I give you company then ",I said.

"Oh really ,I wanted somebody to be with me. Come we will get back by afternoon," He said .

"Wait here I come after informing my parents." I said and moved towards my home.

"Ok I am waiting here but be quick, we have to return also," He said.

After sometime I was on the way to Ghatotand on the bike as a pillion. A host of memories was popping up in my mind .Since the condition of the road was not good we had tough time reaching Ghato and finally school. We were in front of the school gate. The bell for the small break had just gone. Students were out in the assembly ground. He dropped me there and said , "I will get back after two hours".

I said , "Ok, after two hours." I needed time to spend inside the school. I wanted to relive some good moments, spent there. I informed the man at the gate. He asked me the reason of my visit. In those days there was no security guard who would take the signature of the visitor. I went straight into the staff room. I noticed some students were excited as they had recognized me .In the staff room I found most of the teachers were acquainted to me. They threw a cordial welcome. Since it was short break time, teachers stayed there for some time and went to their classes. I went to the back ground, some senior students were playing cricket. They invited me to play. They knew that I played cricket. When I was in the school they were in eight or nine std. I started playing with them. In the mean time Sr.Principal called me through the peon. She had been informed by somebody. I went to the principal's chamber. She asked me to come in.

" Hello Qamar! How are you?" She said smilingly.

"I am good sister. How are you all?" I said.

"We all are fine here ."She replied.

"What brought you here Qamar?". She said.

"Actually a friend of mine was coming here .I thought to meet you all."I said.

"What are you doing nowadays?" She said.

"Preparing for the competitive exams." I answered.

"You were in Delhi I think. When did you get back from there?". She said.

"Last December only .I thought there would be vacancies in the new born state."I said.

"See Qamar , There is a vacancy of an English Language teacher here. If you are interested , you can join. Since you have worked here and understand work culture and staff here ,it will be easy for you to adjust." She put a proposal .Her demeanour was quite convincing and friendly. On the way to her chamber I had thought that she would object to my playing with the students without her permission.

"Sister I shall talk to my parents then I will let you know." I replied.

"Oh yes ,one more thing. You are preparing for the competitive exams that you can continue after joining the school also. You will be engaged in the first half only. The whole second half will be at your disposal. That you can use for yourself." She said ,trying to convince me.

"Ok sister I will leave now. My friend must be waiting outside." I sought permission and left the chamber. I came to the main gate. My friend had reached.

"When did you come here ?" I said

"Five minutes before." He said

We reached home quite on time. In the evening I informed my family about the offer. Mother was not ready. Father was leaving on me. The ball was thrown in my court. Then my eldest brother said, "The timing, you said, is good for you. You can use the second half for the preparation of exams you aim at." At last my father reluctantly agreed on the point.

After three days I got a call from the sister principal. By then I had made up my mind. She asked me whether I had talked to my parents. I told her about my decision. She asked me to join from 1rst Oct.2001.

The decision to join the school was neither a part of my career plan nor was it passion driven. I had nothing concrete in my mind. I decided to join because I was to do something which would give answer to those people who were always ready with the question about my career and suggestions for the same. That at one point of time had become depressive.

This happens especially when we find our goal scattered .We lack single minded devotion for one specific goal. We get carried away with whatever comes on the way. To withstand any such force we must have crystal clear goal, pillared by passion and interest.

PART II

CHAPTER NINE

A DIFFERENT BALL GAME

Finally I came out to join the school .This was the second inning which life was asking me to start, without much idea about this different wicket ,I was going to bat on and ball at. I was to play with the little experience I was going to gain on the daily bases. I didn't carry any big bag or bedding .I came to bus stand .I had no idea about the timing of the buses. I was suggested to go to taxi-stand nearby. When I reached , there was one matador for Ghatotand. It was about to leave. Passengers sitting, somehow made room for me. I reached school and reported to the principal. She was glad to see me. A peon was asked to show me my accommodation. It was the same supervisor 3BHk flat where I had stayed during my first staying. I was given the middle room. The balcony room was already occupied. There was a kitchen and I was entitled to use that. However I was not allowed .My flatmate was a senior teacher. He had been close to Narendra. His behaviour was strange. I realized that when other part of the body is poisoned that can be treated but if ears are poisoned ,it takes years to cure. I could relate the whole thing with my previous stay.

Actually when I left school last time Mr. Narendra stayed here for couple of years and then he had joined a school nearby. He had been close to some of the teachers ,including my flatmate.

If we judge somebody through the eyes of others , our judgement lacks rationale or justified points. We develop preconceived notion about the person. And on most of the occasion when we have first-hand experience with the person , the notion gets shattered.

I dropped the idea of preparing meal. I talked to the owner of a small dhaba kind of hotel. He got ready to serve me lunch and dinner. And for boiling milk and preparing tea I bought a heater and got a switch fixed at one corner of my room. That corner was my make shift kitchen.

Now breakfast was still a question for me. Commonly in the middle class society male members are not even encouraged to learn some of the very common breakfast item like sandwiches ,bread and omelettes etc. I was not exception I would carry biscuits to school for breakfast. I was offered a piece of bread by Mr.J.A.Ansari ,a senior mathematics teacher. I witnessed some teachers covering their breakfast during the break time. Except for few, sharing was not in the culture of the staff room. Two or three days had passed , Mr.Narendra came to meet me at my quarter.

"I heard you have joined Holy Cross". He said.

"Yes, I have." I answered.

"You know I left the school because of the irrational behaviour of the principal." He was giving explanation of his leaving school. Although I was not interested in listening to him.

"Oh!" I exclaimed

"You should not have joined .It would have been a lesson for the principal." He further said. This is typical human psychology when we have problem with somebody we want everybody to have problem with him.

I kept mum .I didn't want to give any explanation. He kept justifying his leaving Holy Cross. He was all praise for his new school and freedom of work he had got there. He was also making fun of the teacher, whom I shared quarter with. Actually he had come to meet him. After that he visited couple of time and disappeared for good.

I was regular in school. In fact I was enjoying teaching. And at the same time I was getting exposed to my ignorance and so many other aspects of teaching and learning process. In schools new teachers are tested by the senior students. In senior classes students ask tricky questions sometime even out of the book. If the teachers answer them smartly they get impressed and stop testing.

In the normal phase of new teachers' journey in a new school, their ability to communicate proves to be handy. It is the most important tool, through which teachers can withstand all the challenges, thrown on them initially. After that the thing which impresses the students the most is –their not carrying many notebooks or books in the classroom. The general reaction of the students is 'they teach so well without books'. If the teacher relates the contents of the book with the current happenings around , they keep the mind of the students in the classroom. Appearance of teachers which include dress-sense , gait and their demeanour ,are also part of a good presentation. Each passing day was a new experience for me.

Coming from the schooling background where girls could not have been imagined even in dream in those days and being unaware of the co-education ,I was , perhaps moving recklessly. I was not aware of slam-book culture. Students often asked me to fill their slam-book. Since I was getting positive response from the students ,I used to share knowledge whatever the little I had ,with them ,whenever I found time. My general knowledge, whatever the little I had it was due the preparation for the competitive examinations, including sports, especially cricket, was proving to be good reasons for the students to be at ease with my presence.

One day I played cricket with the students in their games period ,in my free period. I had class in the next period in XI std. After the bell I went straight away to the class .En-route in the corridor ,I picked a water-bottle of a student and took a few sips. I didn't know it was unusual .Next day in the staff room a teacher was discussing with other teachers. I heard him say, "Qamar sir drinks water from girls' water-bottle". This was very painful for me. That teacher could have told me. Later the same teacher was quoted as saying , he(me) while teaching ,walks in the classroom ,putting his hands into the pocket of his jeans'. Now what was wrong in that I didn't know. By now one thing was clear that some teachers were not comfortable with my presence among the students out-side the class-room. Although I was never told anything by the then principal. As the principal who had appointed me was transferred. Having heard all the gossips I went to the principal and said , "Teachers are making unnecessary comments on me at my back,I don't know how to respond."

"Did I say anything to you?" She said.

"No, but sister!" I said. I couldn't explain my emotion to her.

"But what? Concentrate on your teaching. Study more and enjoy your teaching." She said smiling.

Senior leader or principal like her is an asset for an Institution. She had a unique way to deal with her teachers. She made every teaching or non-teaching staff feel very close to her. She never slapped her leadership on anybody. Hers was the way which would make us realize our little contribution to the overall development of the school. Especially after the Board Exams and other special occasion like Annual Day .Most of us were excited to go to school. We didn't want Sunday or holiday to come .As long as she was there, we teachers always had something new and exciting to do for the students. Teachers had complete liberty to make their teaching useful and interesting for the students. Although session was packed with cultural activities but not at the cost of our academics. In spite of parents' complaint she never compromised with her idea of imparting education.

Since I was close to the students, they often shared their views about their teachers. Later I understood that some did it prepensely to build their image In front of the teachers. They did it with all the teachers. Even wishing teachers, for some ,had a purpose. I noticed with the change in the section ,they changed their direction of wishing. For some the teachers who didn't teach them, they didn't deserve to be wished. Initially it was disturbing but gradually I became used to it. As there were a good majority of the students who, irrespective of their class and section ,showered their respect on the teachers and they got genuine good wishes from the teachers. In the evening they would come to me to discuss their field of interest especially cricket. In between they would give the update of the happenings of the school.

The way they talked it was clear that they needed counselling regarding their career. Whenever I asked them about their career plan. Their standard answer would be , "Not yet decided sir, it depends on the marks." For me, finding them in the same situation where ,once, I had found myself, it was painful. They needed somebody who would make them explore and them to know their strength and weakness. They needed somebody who would work on their belief system. Now CBSE has integrated career counselling with the year planner.

Till 2004-05, students hardly talked about Kota, JEE, AIEE,NEET,CA,ICWA etc. Students didn't find them gettable. As even the best ones had not made it. Then two students cracked IIT. It was a turning point in the line of thinking of the people.It became table talk in the small township of Ghato. Now people would talk and plan about their wards. Parents had a reference point .There started a rush for Kota, Vizag, Hyderabad etc. for classes cum coaching. The success rate was quite low but it had certainly broadened the view of the parents as well as students.

For me talking to them about their career was a way to escape from loneliness. There was no TV in the room. I had a small transistor for recreation. Every Saturday I could not resist the pleasure of meeting my family members and friends. Once I was at Hazaribagh and there was marriage of one of my cousins. I was asked to stay back and attend the function. Preparation was in full-swing. While talking to elder brother of the cousin sister who was getting married ,he told me about all the petty issues which are unnecessarily stretched out of proportion and many times they prove to be disastrous for the up coming relationship. Marriage in our community is a contract ,signed ,in front of two respected and reliable witness. But now it has been made a mega event. All the peripheral activities, which have crept in due the assimilation of different cultures, have made the whole event so expensive that bride's parent have to struggle to meet the expenditure. Consequently many girls are not married in their right time.

All these could have been made very simple as they are advised but due to so many factors, mostly social, they turn out to be a herculean and knotty task for bride's parents .It starts with the paying a visit to each other house. It is meant to know and understand each other but it becomes an opportunity for some, from both the sides, mostly bridegrooms' side, to find hole in their coat. The parents of the bride groom or sometime brides' take rear seat and relatives, who had never been seen associated with them in the past, all of a sudden become fragile objects, which needed very careful handling .At the end of the day it is found that marriage has been made a multi-dimensional social event, a time it is a show off time, a competition of proving oneself wealthier, a time to display social status etc. And in the existing social situation havenots are always at the receiving end. Had the marriage been held as it has been told in the religious books, no young girl would have stayed in their home unmarried.

The marriage got over .Thankfully nothing unwanted happened. Everything went well .I had to catch the earliest bus for Charhi and then from there a Treker for Ghato. On the way I saw people with five or six bags of coal on their cycle ,pulling them with their hands, supported by their legs. I could well realize how the burden of life, metaphorically, is borne by a vast majority of the people. This kind of sight gives us a moment to introspect and realize, how good we are! I reached school at around seven fifteen. Almost reporting time for the school.

I went straight to the school. The bell had just gone. I didn't have class in the first period. I started preparing for my class in the second period. Just then a peon came and said , "Sir, sister principal is calling you".

"May I come in sister," I said standing at the gate of the chamber.

"Yes ,Sajid ,come in". She said.

"Tomorrow we have parents Teachers meeting .Since Mr.Chatterjee, class teacher of IX A ,is absent,I want you to show the result to the parents. You teach in the class .You know the students also."

"Ok sister, as you wish." I said.

She rang the bell to call the peon.

"Give the report card and the attendance register of IX A to sir." She said to the peon.

I was given both the things .I kept them in my drawer. Next day when I reached school some parents had already come to see the report card of their wards. They wore their crash helmet and coal dust was there on their faces. We were asked to go to our respective classes. I sat outside the classroom. I was following other teachers.

Parents started coming .Those who had come early in the morning , were in hurry. They wanted to observe formality by putting their signature on the said space and go back home. Actually I was in the impression that there would be a proper meeting with the parents as the name had suggested. They were sleep deprived as they had night-shift-duty. Two parents came I put the report cards after asking the name of their wards. I had no idea about their overall performance. I noticed the parent who was hurrying to sign the report card ,now had sat on the bench ,placed in front of my table.

I said , "What happened?" He didn't say anything and the report card of his ward in front of me. The other one was busy in noting down the marks on a small piece of paper. I looked at the report card. It had red mark in almost all the subject. The parent looked at me. He seemed agonised.

"What more can I do sir? I can't study in his place. I am coming after the night shift duty. I thought to sign the report card first and take rest." He said and was almost in tears .His pain perhaps intensified , seeing the other report card which reflected good marks in all the subjects. After signing the report card he left without uttering a word further.

Next day I was in the same class. I talked about overall performance of the class .I made students clap for the one who had topped in the class. He stood up while students were clapping. He didn't look that happy.

" Are you not happy Nimish?" I said.

"No sir I am not, this time I got two marks lesser than in the previous test." He replied.

"Never mind , dear, next time you will get more ."I said consoling him.

"Yes sir!." He said smiling and sat down.

"How many of you have failed in three or more subjects?" I said to the class.

Around ten students stood up. They seemed indifferent .One of them was the same student whose father had wept the previous day. They were least bothered. Some of them were smiling. It was surprising that in the same class there was a student who in spite of being topper , was not happy because two marks less had mattered to him. And here we had students who had failed in more than three subjects ,were quite unperturbed.

I had the impression that this happens in Govt. School only. I could well recollect that how relaxed my class was even after the pre board exam. A few of us were serious ,that too because of our parents' following up. My father was in the school itself therefore there was no question of dodging or bunking the class. Thanks to my father whose efforts made me top in my school, in the Tenth Board. In the pre board examination I got eighty two in English when I was shown the answer book. Copies were evaluated by Mr. Suleman(late). I was happy as I had fetched good marks in his subject. A day before the result showing my father called me and handed over my answer book to me saying, "See how many mistakes you have made." I looked at the total, eighty two was struck off instead I was given forty two only.

What made me reflect on the fact that there was stark similarities in the demeanour of the students, of my time and of the present time, who had no idea whatsoever ,why they were studying.

Education not only enables people how to earn but also how to live. This becomes crystal clear in our day today interaction with the students. Life does not change in year ,month or days but it changes the moment you decide to change. The seed of the change is sown the moment you have a goal in mind .Furthermore if you stick to it, you have a tunnel vision and you don't have much time to waste. Success is the result of good decision.

In normal circumstances, especially in the Indian sub-continent, teen-agers are not given complete freedom to take decision but their parents, elders or other relatives' views prevail over their decision. Consequently they don't sound or look confident in their approach. They lack interest which results in lacking consistency. Although consistency is the most important ingredient, required in shaping the fate of the students. Interest and consistency is not developed overnight. A very common shortcoming is noticed among majority of the parents that they show their concern only when their ward reach in ninth or tenth. In our time parents hardly bothered when their wards remained in lower classes. However that is the time when interest or inclination for any subject is developed. If the interest gets aligned with the goal, may be short term in early stages, it delivers, in terms of marks, consequently developing a sense of competition. It bears fruit in the long run.

No successful person has ever been born whose purpose of life was not clear. Our talent, time, intelligence, labour strife, emotions or sacrifices are of no use unless these are guided by a purpose. we can't imagine a football match without a goal post. Intense love or fascination for the set goal enables a person to change their desires into dream and dream into reality.

Sometime we have goal, but that remains blurred. Consistency in approach removes the mist that surrounds it. Our goal should be well defined. Initially along with the actual target, we see all the peripheral objects in the frame. But as we concentrate, those unwanted objects start getting eliminated. And finally we have the tunnel vision of the target. We may have some examples-

I have to get good marks-Vague, not specific.

I have to get 95% marks-Well defined.

Our goal should be under our control not others-

Eg-I want to make my son clear NEET-(Not under our control). The success of my son depends on the effort he makes. I can't put in effort on his behalf. Our goal should be based on the positive thoughts. Negativity always brings conditions and other weed like ideas with the set target. These weeds need to be weeded out, the earliest the better. The more specific we are about our goals the more enthusiastic we find ourselves ,thinking about the accomplishment of the same. **Napolean Hill says, "Man can achieve anything which they can clearly think of."**

It was painful to see students making mistakes in prioritizing their activities. Education didn't come anywhere at the top. Ours was more critical time.We hardly found anybody planning for post tenth board steps.

I was so obsessed with playing cricket that I took admission in Zila School 10+2 although I could have taken admission in good colleges .I wanted to play inter-school cricket. This I did at the cost of my studies. No classes were held at the zila School. I didn't know where the classrooms were. And I was perfectly ok with it.

Perhaps I was not able to put myself in the shoes of those who had gone through the similar situation and then they were nowhere. I saw a flickering light of hope, could be unrealistic, somewhere and I chased recklessly.

Here in the school I found majority of the students with no specific goal whatsoever. Although in this township people didn't have much to do after their duty. After politics and some current social issues, they had, the career planning of their wards, to discuss. Their seriousness had no match with that of their wards, in most of the cases. They sounded as if their suppressed passionate desire, getting echoed in their words. They wanted to realize their dream by seeing their wards excel in the field of Engineering or Medicals. The negative part of this aspect was most of them were obsessed with Engineering Degree for their wards. There were students, who never passed in Mathematics and Physics, were admitted in private

Engineering Colleges. Any how they became Engineer but didn't get good placement. Once I met a parent. I said to him , "Where is your son now?" I knew he had B-Tech degree from a private unknown college.

"Sir, he got a job in Banglore. He was getting twenty thousand. Every month he asked for money as accommodation and foods were too costly for him to meet the expenses along with other sundry expenditure." He said in a very sad tone.

He further added, "When I got him admitted I had thought he would be a helping hand for me. At least he would bear all his expenditure independently. But he was heavily dependent on me. I called him back and asked him to join my small business here."

The same was the case with so many other parents who had no idea about the potentialities of their wards and the condition of job market. They got their wards admitted in the Engineering colleges, after paying a huge donation, without any prior investigation and placement of the college. Some of these colleges have understanding with the companies. They come and recruit candidates in bulk. After a few months they fire those who prove themselves a kind of liability for the companies. Some companies hire them, irrespective of their branch of engineering, and make them sit with the computer and get their work done. After some time the recruited individuals forget their own branch of studies. The colleges do the marketing of their college on the bases of the placement. This becomes the most fascinating factor for the parents and students to take admission in these colleges.

This has been happening for many years. It has become a part of the system. Jobs are less and applicants are more. We have gone far beyond the saying 'survival for the fittest'.

Now whosoever is smarter and fitter than the smartest and fittest survives and comes up with the flying colour.

The process of becoming better than the best starts from the school that too from early classes. It doesn't happen overnight. During these periods students have lots of curiosity and energy for anything and everything.

Once there was dispersal time of a school. A balloon seller was selling balloons. In order to attract the prospect buyers he, time to time released balloon into the air and balloon went up into the sky. Children were getting enchanted towards it and thronging around the balloon seller. After sometime when gathering of the children melted he got ready to collect his things. No sooner the balloon got ready to go than a young black boy came to him and said innocently , "Uncle, if you release that black balloon ,will that also go up, like all other balloons? The balloon seller said, "Son, balloon doesn't fly because of its colour but the gas it has inside it takes to that height."

Children during this phase of life have lots of curiosity and excitement .They can do anything to get things they want. Their courage and ideas need to be winged. Even after growing up they will complain of resources. They will mould the situation in their favour by dint of their will. This is the age when children experience many physical as well as emotion changes in them. They develop their ego, self-respect and attraction towards opposite gender. Here they ought to be handled with lots of care and understanding. Parents and peers play the most important role in shaping their ideas and thoughts about life and career as well. When they find contradiction in what their parents say and what they hear from their peer outside. This is very ticklish situation. If, in this situation parents present themselves as 'must-obey people' who invest their money for their career or have to shoulder responsibility as parents. In other words when they thrust their parenting on them instead of treating them as friends, there are high possibilities of the wards' becoming indifferent to the dream and aspiration of the parents. In some cases wards become emotionally vulnerable. Little sympathy or concern from friends may make them carry away.

But the parents who understand that when father's shoes fit in the feet of the wards, they should be treated as friends, spend quality time with wards which helps in keeping abreast with the physical as well as emotional development of the child. Not only this, parents get plenty of chances to bejewel the thoughts and ideas of the child with the required values ,which in the long run help them to resist the flood of temptations to get lost in the hedonistic world. It also helps them in coping the stress which are inevitable on the way to achieve the set goal. It doesn't let the ambition get unbridled. The studded values make them resilient and develop perseverance in them .These 'must have qualities' help them in staying grounded in all different situations .In success or failure ,they neither become success intoxicants nor heart broken ,to the extent of taking some fatal steps.

Knute Rockne said, "When the going gets tough, the tough get going." When situations are tough, the tough rise to the occasion .They set example for others by surviving and winning at the end.

Robert H. Schuller has compared people with potatoes. When potatoes are harvested they are spread out and sorted out according to their size. There were two farmers .One made effort to segregate potatoes according to their size. After that it would be easy for him to sell in the market. The other went straight to the market from his field in his wagon. He would reach early and therefore make more money. This puzzled the first farmer. "How do you do it?" He said to the second farmer. He said, "I just load the wagon with potatoes and take the roughest road to the market. During the transportation, the little potatoes always fall to the bottom, the medium potatoes land in the middle while the big potatoes rise to the top."

This is what applicable in our life. The way big potatoes rise to the top, going through rough roads, tough (mentally) people rise to the top, going through tough situations.

School has a pivotal role to play in designing the thought and ideas of the students. It has to be inclusive of all that are required in the holistic development of the students. The very design should be based on the inclination, noticed at the early age when they are in six or seven. Although their priority keeps changing, depending upon the environment they are exposed to. One day I was in class seven. I was asking about the career options .One boy said, "I want to be a signal man in Railway." I don't know how on Earth he thought of that job. "Why do you think of that job? I questioned. "I saw it on the Television, sir." He replied. "You ought to think something big like Medical, Engineering, Civil services etc."I mentioned those options since I knew he was a very sincere student. I was told that his father didn't have proper income. They had been going through lots of financial constraint. That never reflected on his façade. He was all excited to learn.

When students have enough, available at their homes, they lack the willingness to have achievements, of his own, in his bag. Their comforts restrict them, in most of the cases, from pushing their limitations. Nothing is pressing for them. Exceptions are always there. There are some who don't let their comfort, made available by parents, make them complacent. Their love for somebody, may be their parents , friends ,anger against an individual or deep seated will to prove themselves ,becomes the propelling force which make them turn all their obstacles into stepping stones. Dsarath Manjhi, the mountain man, tore mountain into two part making a passage to go through the mountain. He had seen his wife go around the same mountain to fetch water. It was his love for his wife made him do this herculean task.

The process of larvae's coming out of cacoon and becoming a beautiful butterfly offers a great learning to us. Nothing big can be achieved without coming out of the comfort zone. Students have to be prepared for the challenges and the cut throat competition, the world offers to them, when they go out of their home, leaving all the care of mother and concern of father.

Students have two births one the biological the other when they understand the purpose of their birth. The meaning of the purpose varies and many factors contribute to it. After parents, School being the most important place where they have their friends and teachers whose influence, may be little, is inescapable .Their socio-economic condition has also an important role to play. The sooner they realize and rationalize it the bigger the goal they achieve. Such students don't let the current trend influence their career choice. They discover their forte and the very discovery manifests in their tirelessness in studying a subject or doing a very specific thing may be experiment or playing with tools or paint brush. Then they free themselves from time and space. The very freedom makes them forget time and place when they find themselves in their study or work place.

Every action needs a threshold force. Every successful person has a reference point to tell that when exactly the idea of achieving that goal took shape in their mind. Most of the time an appreciation or a reward or trust placed by parents etc. prove to be that point. This gives an ignition or spark to the 'will to do' element. It often happens during the schooling days. Therefore school is the place which should provide a very fertile ground to the seeds of new thought and ideas, the students come with. A healthy environment gives impetus to the growth of the same ,resulting in the holistic development of the students thereby building a strong foundation for the future society and nation.

In the present education system the impact of the result oriented approach can be noticed very easily. Marks have replaced all other purposes of education wherein it is found that students' as well teachers' effort revolve around marks. And in this pursuit the real purpose of education seems to have lost. What has added salt to injury is, the professionalism on the part of the teacher and materialism on the students. There started the mushrooming of the coaching centres and private tuitions. This has affected the relationship between the teachers and the students. Furthermore it has impacted the ambience of the teaching and the learning process of the school. Marks are the ultimate yardsticks to judge the ability of the students as well as the teachers. At least at the school level for sure. Students are not ready to study beyond the syllabi, prescribed for them and teachers are not ready to take pain to go beyond their assigned syllabi.

Over the years CBSE has smoothed the ground for the teachers to give marks to the brim by bringing about frequent changes in the pattern and the marking scheme of the examination. Since it is easy to fetch 70% to 80% without much effort. Students don't need to burn midnight oil except those who have a well-defined goal. They hardly take thing seriously .In our time there would be an atmosphere all around for the Board examinee. At every corner there would be somebody who would say, "You have board exam this year! Go home and study." At home we would get long lecture, if found outside. Father said, "Don't take X board exam casually. It is the first and most important gate of your career." There existed third division. First division was a matter of pride not only for parents but for the whole mohallah. Every-one in the mohallah showed concern for the board examinee. Any uncle of Mohalla could scold and ask the appearing candidate about their preparation. The best part of our time was that no one would mind seeing their son or daughter getting scolding by any other person of the mohallah. Rather they would feel obliged to them. This approach of the society has disappeared. Now forget colony or mohallah people ,next door neighbour can't do this. They(students) would not be expected outside their home, three or four months before the exam. Now that seriousness is matter of far cry even a week before the examination. Thanks to new policy of CBSE. In normal circumstances we hid our punishment in the school from our parents ,as there was possibility of getting more by them. They would justify the punishment by teacher by either scolding or beating . Now that scope has been finished by laws. Teachers' hands have been tied up. Forget beating, teachers can't scold students . We are warned by our authority repeatedly about any-thing that may touch the tender, soft and pampered mind and heart of the students. However, we are held responsible for their heart and mind being devoid of the required sensitivity and empathy, when they go out from the school and participate in the social and economic proceeding of the country.

As I was spending more time with students , hence many unacknowledged aspects of the teachers' and students' relationship were coming up. One common thing between students, teachers and parents' relationship was that they wanted to be understood from their position and with their ideas and beliefs only. Although little change or adjustment may make thing easy for every-one. Things have changed very fast in the last three decades. But the fundamental of human nature has not changed. Love and compassion had changed a dacoits into a sage. The same is bond to change a brat into a brilliant student. Dialogue and counselling are still the best way as far as managing students is concerned.

Ours was the time when professionalism was still at the periphery of the teachers' domain. We were not only touched by them academically but emotionally also. I am reminded of teachers, after my father, Dhananjay Pratap Singh, who taught us science. He was an example of gentlemanliness. Jawed Abdullah, he was an obscured gem of knowledge of his subject(Arabic).Whoever had will ,they could have plenty from him. Later during my masters I was lucky to get the tutelage of Mr. R.N. Jha sir, who was compassion personified .He made us understand what should be our approach towards educators and educands. His was the house which could be called 'modern gurukul'.We had free access to his kitchen. We felt like a part of his family. He ruled the heart of the students. He used to say, "There was big communication gap between our teachers and us. We could not think of going to our teacher and ask any doubts. We ran pillar to post to get the same cleared. I thought if I became a teacher I would finish the gap. Students will have no fear or inhibition whatsoever in coming to me with their queries." We experienced that he did more than what he thought and said.

Every school is expected to provide **three C's** to the students –**Confidence, Creativity** and **Character.** The school ought to provide a conducive atmosphere to the students wherein they realize their individuality and develop a strong belief system. This starts from the classroom. When a teacher encourages students to raise questions and that are followed by appreciation, it opens up avenues for the students to embark on a journey of self-realisation. It ends up in making them know their innate talent and set goal in their life.

The second important contribution of the school ought to make in students' life is to create an ambience wherein they independently form their own idea, not only of the world they live in but the one which is beyond their reach. Their fertile mind should be watered to form ideas and thoughts, needed for the development of the society and the country at large. This independence of free thinking helps them in exploring all the possibilities of the betterment of the human being.

After having confidence and fruitful thought , students need a strong value system which enables them to develop empathy for the needy ,to understand the importance of relationship , the place of parents ,friends and teachers in their life. The third 'C' is character building .When a young kids step into the school , they are like lump of clay. Teachers have to give them shape. The shape heavily depends on the way teachers handle them. Each scolding and appreciation ought to chip out the unwanted edges of the students' personality. Punishment works, provided they need to be convinced about the reason for the same.

Here the emotional growth of the students should not be ignored. Because devoid of the emotional strength they may not resist the temptation and withstand the challenges the world throws at them at every step. Sometime an emotionally weak individual succumb to a small difficulties or challenges of life. Therefore what psychologist and educationist think is that a student ought to be appreciated in front of the whole class whereas punished alone.

The education, being imparted in all different institutions, involves , bipolar process ,wherein one pole is 'educands' while the other is 'educator'. Both the poles have a social and economical background they come from. They have their own mind-set and challenges in their life. Without addressing those challenges neither of them can come up to the expectations of all the stake holders. To understand the emotional side of the students we have 'counselling classes' for the students. Expertise are invited to do the counselling of the students. It brings forth the result in most of the cases. But the educators and the support staff are treated as machine which have an 'Off' and 'On' switch. They are supposed to switch the 'on' button for the school after stepping into it, and switch off the button for all that he leaves at their home. In many schools teachers are not allowed to carry mobile phones into the school. Although carrying mobile phone into the classroom is not a good idea, except with a special purpose. Some schools ask their teachers to submit their mobile phones at the gate only. They are expected to maintain a positive demeanour even if they have problems at their home.

In the condition mentioned above , principal has to play an important role. When I joined school ,I couldn't help feeling , 'I Came ,I Saw and I Was Conquered '.The senior leaders were so understanding that we felt like home in the school. We didn't have AC in the staff room but we used to chill .Teaching was a wonderful experience for us. We had tremendous amount of 'sense of belonging' for the school. Everything was going smoothly. But what begins has to end.

There came a news of joining a new principal. Under the present principal, Sr.Usha, years had rolled down like months. Perhaps our complacency had made us feel like this. We didn't get tired of doing work in the school. We didn't mind spending extra hour in the school. Every day was a new day, packed with enthusiasm and excitement for us. And all these had been possible because of our Sr.principal.

CHAPTER TEN

A WHIRLWIND

Finally the formal announcement of the farewell of the principal was made. We were as sad as sad we could be. Some teachers wept in the principal chamber. Couple of days before the summer vacation she visited our quarter. This was the old practice of the out-going principal.

After the vacation we joined school with lots of curiosity to know who was our new principal but to our utter surprise , a sister who had joined as an English Language teacher, had been promoted as the new head of the school. The apprehension about the principal was no more. She had enough idea of the functioning of the school. We had no intuition of the beginning of an unprecedented bizarre period of the school. Initially things looked normal. But gradually changes started in everything. We were used to having principal as the ultimate head in the hierarchy. But now we had another one who had been given almost all power .He was literally a de-facto principal. Other senior most teachers, who had standing of more than 25 years in the school ,were forced to dance at his tune. An unsaid line was drawn between them at the top, with few of their 'yes persons' and rest of the teaching and non- teaching staff. The de facto principal had a well cushioned chair to sit separately. Teachers had to take permission before stepping into his chamber (computer lab).

He, the self-styled second man in the school, had introduced a system of upgrading the teaching and learning process, designed by TATA STEEL,TQMS, for the company. He would often go to Jamshedpur, for the training for the same. In the guise of upgrading the school he was leaving no opportunities to upgrade himself. His words were words, spoken by the principal. Many teachers had surrendered before him. They didn't want any hassle in their life. But some senior teachers whose spine was too strong to be bent, found it had to adjust with this weird functioning of the school. When they voiced their concern they were humiliated in front of junior teachers. Some teachers had found out way how to appease him. They did it by making his kids appear in almost all the cultural programme, especially in dance wherein they remained at the centre throughout the programme. Other dancers stayed at the back. This was there in spite of all murmuring and comments of the parents. His kids were the only kids who could offer bouquet to the guests, who visited on all the important occasions.

Power pampers, absolute power makes people look down upon others. One day a colleague of mine met me in the evening .He was looking unusually sad. "You are looking off colour today, what happened?", I said. He had been giving his all out to the school. He had been on the duty to serve the second man of the school. One day he went in the evening but was not seen by him. His half day salary was deducted. Although his effort could be seen in the over all development of the student in the sporting activities. But all were of no values as he was seen spending time with us. "As you know there is marriage of my brother at Hazaribagh. I went to give her(Sister principal) invitation card." He said.

"Then what happened?", I said.

"She didn't take the card saying, how dare you give me this card!," He said.

It was shocking for me. What made her do this, I still don't get the answer of this question. But I had seen him (my colleague) in agony. He had experienced how a person, after getting power for few years , consider themselves superior to the rest , who are around. This high handedness went on increasing. I was 15 August. Preparation had been completed. On the very day sister principal was out .Three bouquet had been ordered .One for the chief guest , one for the principal and one for the sister who was in the senior wing. Now who would receive the bouquet in the sister's absence, was question. We the cultural in-charges asked the senior most teacher, Mr.R.D.Sharma to receive the same. The programme got over .Everything went well. The chief guest was all praise for the programme. After two days sister principal got back. A meeting was called in the staff room .We thought she would talk about the programme. But she said , "Mr. Sharma you have great fascination for bouquet." We all were looking at each other. Perhaps Mr Sharma didn't understand the irony of the sentence. He smiled.

"How dare you receive the bouquet, meant for the principal." She thundered in the staff room. Mr. Sharma was speechless. "Sorry, Sister! He said apologetically. But she didn't stop. She went on insulting him mercilessly. Now she was targeting all those who had refused to bow down before Mr. second, one by one. A senior most teacher who had been teaching in higher classes was given lower classes to teach. A very common act of vengeance by the principal.

I was teaching English Core in XII. In that year the result of English was the best ever. Out of 42 students 29 had got 90% or more than 90%.I was not given XII class for the next session. Senior teachers were not ready to stoop low to be in their good book. Now it was S. S. Singh who was made to say sorry to a student in front of whole class. He had slapped one student who was fighting in his class. Actually that boy, after fighting in the class, went to the principal chamber and from there a scene was created to make other believe that he (S.S. Singh) had done a great wrong to the boy. Later he was taken to the hospital to get his ears checked up. A good drama was orchestrated by the two bosses to demoralize him.

In a small township like Gahtotand, people didn't have many issues to disscuss. Till the media and social media had not started catering all concocted stuff to serve their own purpose ,forgetting their responsibility as one of the strongest pillars of democracy. Parents started talking about the super duo of the school. Even in the school campus students were found commenting on this. We were mute spectators now. Each passing day gave us a sigh of relief with some apprehension about the next day .We were mentally prepared to face an issue ,designed to let us down and silence us from voicing against all , that were happening in name of appraisal and development.

The best thing of the school was the undeterred teaching spirit of the teachers. We never let our teaching get affected because of the circumstance, we had been catapulted in. We, at no cost , wanted our students to suffer. This was paying off. The result of X and XII Board had been outstanding. Perhaps this had made the parents and other stake holders keep mum. Apparently it seemed 'ALL IZ WELL'. But by the end of her fourth year of her regime about fourteen teachers had resigned .Some of them could have been a big asset for the school.

In such a situation we needed somebody who could understand our emotions. The students who had seen our hay days in the school often asked about school. We didn't speak much but to some we, especially ,I could not help speaking a little. One day , Narita, our student rang me up. She too had some questions for which I had no answer. She was all concerned for the school. During her schooling she was exemplary as a student. Hers was the classic example of the saying , 'work hard so silently that success should be heard from kilometre'. Her result in the X Board had translated that saying into a reality. In her class there was a girl who never stood second in her class from her lower classes. It was the result of the X board .She, along with her parents, looked and sounded confident. She even sometime sounded overconfident .But Narita maintained low profile. On being asked about the result she smiled and allowed other to speak. Result was announced and that over-confident girl was no-where in the top ten rank holders of the school. Narita emerged as a topper. On that day I understood that success is a sum total of many things, including our behaviour, demeanour and overall approach toward people who are around.

Narita, after talking for some time said, "Tomorrow I am going to come to you .I have to show you something."

"Great, Come I will wait, " I said. Next day she was at my quarter with a bunch of printed sheets. She gave me and said, "Do read sir, and give me your comment."

"Yes sure!" I said ,taking those papers .On that day she didn't mention anything about her writing.

After a few days I got a call from Narita.

"Did you read those papers sir?" She said.

"Yes a few pages not the whole. Quite impressive dear!" I said. Although I had read too less to make any comment. The front page bore the title 'Fire in the Belly'. After that I forgot about the papers as I got busy in the correction of answer books and all the documentation works which remained in full swing in those days.

After a month Narita again came to me with an invitation of the 'Book Release Function' ,scheduled on the next day, of her book 'Fire in the Belly'. The stapled papers had become a book .Now the book had the title 'Fire in The Belly, Do You Feel It by Narita. To my utter amazement she had dedicated that book me and her family .I was overwhelmed to have been given such a pedestal by my student. I didn't know how to react. She had mentioned the reason of her dedication of the book to me. The other day I was there at the Auditorium with her family members and other invited guests, including our principal, on the stage. This was the first time I was witnessing a book release function. And on being part of it ,gave a different feelings, which can't be justified by words. All the important Tata officials and pressmen were there. I found my principal and her deputy were talking to one reporter whom the deputy was introducing himself as the vice principal of the school. Although there is no official position of a vice principal in the school.

In such a situation of despair and hopelessness , this came as a huge moral booster for me. This was one of the rarest returns one can expect as a teacher from a student. That too in a school. Such a moment of pleasure and satisfaction I had never expected. Especially in a time when the leader and her aid were not leaving a single stone unturned to target our efficiency and discredit us. This was a silver line in the cloud for the much awaited good days.

The whole episode had consolidated my belief that if you are honest in putting in effort in whatever the field you belong to ,that effort will bear fruit later or sooner. In case of teaching, a teacher uses all their ability for all the students. Making use of the stuff, taught in the classroom ,depends on the individual approach. There is a poem 'Confession of a Born Spectator' by Ogden Nash. In the poem the poet confesses the he is glad neither to be an athlete nor ant sports person. In such a situation of complacency no motivation or inspiration works. Cheerleaders or cheering up gives motivation to those who are on the field not to those who enjoy popcorn sitting at the gallery. Yes there are always cases that young people get motivated ,seeing their role model ,receive accolades and trophies. Michael Phelps created history in the world of swimming. His swimming inspired many young swimmers who are all set to make their presence felt in world arena of swimming. One such was a young boy, who once watched Phelps as an spectator and later he competed with Phelps .And not only competed ,he defeated him in the sports where he had ruled for many years. Therefore the seed of willingness is the first and foremost condition to have a plant of success. A little interest brings you close to that point where motivation starts acting upon. It happens irrespective of the place and social position.

Narita 's example is relevant in two ways. A strong belief in oneself , coupled with hard work, without much tom-toming ,makes you walk on the untrodden path successfully. Second, words of inspiration inspire those who have elements to be inspired. Rain falls at all different kind of land but only the fertility of the land makes use of the rain and brings forth plants. A teacher tells so many things in the class .Very few students show manifestations of the said things. Here the 'readiness to accept' works in the students. Teachers in the school get chance to touch the life of the students .Especially in the lower classes when their mind remain impressionable. In these classes teachers are the ultimate persons to be heard and followed ,for the students. However the very idea keeps undermining as they move to upper classes.

Couple of harsh winters passed and there came a spring. The leadership of the school changed. And the reason which brought about the change was the event ,considered by them to be the most historic for the Holyen of Ghato. Perhaps this is how God plans and His way of execution often comes as a surprise.

CHAPTER ELEVEN

LESSONS LEARNT

Life teaches us every moment. Numerous of people who apparently look quite successful as they have money, assets, power, prestige, social status, and every kind of convenience nevertheless they are disappointed and restless from within. Actually the reward of success is the realisation .A realization which encompasses peace of mind and feelings of ones own value. People in the mad race of earning money , forget that these feelings and realization can not be bought.

There is a balance in everything , created by God in the universe. Little disturbance in the balance of celestial bodies will lead to complete peril. We the human beings have to maintain a balance among different departments of our life in order to have a happy life. They are- a)Health b) Spirituality c)Finance d)Family e)Career f)Self g)Services.

If we don't maintain balance among these, we can't realize the real meaning of success. Our best time is that what we spend with our family. Our family has maximum right on us. Today if at all we talk about stress and its consequences in our life ,it is because of not maintaining balance among the mentioned departments or aspects of life.

We need worldly wisdom to have balance in our life. Present day syllabi can not instil the needed wisdom .Family and society together can create an environment wherein students can learn the subtle practical points of life. Our forefather didn't know about stress management. They were not devoid of stress but they knew how to manage it by their own. The young ones were not told ,they learnt ,looking at their old ones.

Consistency in learning and knowing life is the foremost condition to reach to the goal, "The way a dying man has desire to live more, Socrates says that he has the same amount of desire of learning". We have to learn that people's opinion about life is based on their personal experience and feelings which they gain during their life. It naturally varies person to person.

All the successful people of the world have consistency in their approach. 'Nothing is free in this world'. Even for begging one has to trample ones self-respect. On the way of being consistent there may be obstacles and each obstacle tests our courage and even sometime compels us to crush our desire and hobby. Loosing courage to face difficulty is failure. Hero is the person who, in every condition, remains firm and consistent in his effort to reach to the goal. He believes in Almighty and seeks help from Him. Had success come to the people without failure, all those who made attempt would have been successful. Everything which a person gets after making effort is costly and valuable. Difficult situation polishes the personality of successful people. They are like Tea bag .Its taste is acknowledged and appreciated only when it is dipped in hot water. We cannot judge their talent unless they are put in boiled water(Tough situation).

Everybody dreams while sleeping but the dream which keeps you waking up brings success. Most of the people waste their energy in problem even they become part of it. Very few concentrate on the solutions. Solutions come when peripheral objects are blurred and solution becomes the nucleus of our sight. Every winner has a vision consequently they eye at future. The failures keep lamenting about the past. If we get lessons from the past ,it helps in shaping success in the present .

The people who progress, concentrate on those things which are under their control and they can change those things. They don't give any consideration to things like complexion, race, birth, parents, past mistakes, situation of the country, instead they work very hard on their attitude, belief system, education and some special potential if any. Therefore success is not a matter of chance but a matter of choice. Hellen Keller said, "Nature has done many wrong to me but I don't have time to think what I have not been given." If we don't want to change our condition no one in this world can change.

We live in a strange world where everyone wants to become rich but they hate the rich. People amass wealth for their safety but they end up doing safety for their wealth. Wealth is a need to satisfy worldly desire. If it comes through fair means there nothing wrong in it .But having avarice for it creates path of corruptions. There is harsh reality of life that flow of wealth makes us forget others and lack of wealth makes other forget us.

Before we come out to conquer the world we will have to conquer ourselves. And in the process our thought plays a pivotal role. Our thoughts are more powerful than our emotions and feelings. Our thought helps us in exploring our values, inclination and preferences. These are the ingredients which, ultimately, are used in the recipe of success. According to a research 'in the success of a person, their intelligence contributes only 16% rest 84% is caused by our values, inclination and preferences'.

If we want to change our emotion and feelings we will have change our values. When cause is changed, result automatically gets changed. If a person is ignoring us it does not mean he doesn't respect us but we are not bringing change which he wants to see in us and hear from us. If our values are clear our knowledge and practice will be same.

We humans are by nature impatient .When we are children we are desperate to grow young and when the responsibilities of worldly affair fall on us, we shed tears remembering our childhood. Without effort we grow young and then slip into the evening of life. Time does not stay. We have to keep pace with time. We ought to make our ways simple and straight. Complexities in thought and actions bear undesired result. If railway tracks don't move in straight path they will not be able to bear the weight of the trains and help them reach to their destination.

Advices prove to be fruitful when the receiver is interested in it. The interest of the listener gives strength to the speaker. Four to five decades back speakers used to speak on the bases of their first-hand experience of their life and a few examples from pages of history. Now we have their experiences in the shape of books. They inspire us. They make us reflect upon our life and the life of the people around. We can relate those said or written ideas of life with that of ours. We often come across people with the following statements-

a) In the present scenario one can't get a govt. job without any recommendation.

b) Everyone is selfish here.

c) There is scarcity of good people.

d) One can succeed only if fate favours.

e) There is no value of the honest.

These are the results of our one way approach towards people. We have great deal of anticipation from the people around. Although anticipation is that path through which we form a very narrow idea after having references from the few sources available to us.

It is our attitude which makes the big difference. This is what decides our ALTITUDE. The richest man in the world takes the same space while sleeping and has the same amount of time in a day what a beggar takes and has. The manifestation of this Attitude is seen when we see people 'Strongly Mental' and getting rejected from the society and the same society producing 'Mentally Strong' people, beating all odds and reaching to the top. It is our attitude which leads to Hopeless End and the same instils Endless Hope.

Our ideas and thoughts can be guessed through our words but before that what is seen is more important. Socrates said, 'Strong minds discuss ideas, Average minds discuss events and Weak minds discuss people.'

Problem is a sign of life. Dead people don't have problem. Stress is natural to human beings. In most of the cases it is a must for performance. It becomes problem when we over-rate or under-rate it. It happens when we mix up our priorities. When, what is, important is ignored it becomes urgent. Hence when health is ignored for long time, its related issues reach to the point of urgency. We have to keep reminding ourselves and pray -

- To accept the things that we can't change,
- That we all are free to have our choices

- To seek wisdom to judge what I can and what I can't.
- To give the ability to convert the wasted time into productive time.
- To make you so strong that crisis should not define you but it should refine you .
- To be able to build positive relationship
- To be able to understand that helping each other ought to be the duty of friendship not the purpose.

Going through the process of introspection, consequently bringing about the required change in the attitude makes a personality. Although the word personality has been derived from the Greek word, Persona which means mask. In Greek, theatre artist used to wear the mask of different character, suitable to the occasion and story. When we talk about personality what we mean is the conduct, behaviour ,language and other visible trait of a person. What is hidden such as confidence ,belief system ,determination ,will-to-do etc. are the individuality of a person. Personality can be spiffed up, decorated, made presentable. Like a tree the visible part may be trimmed or pesticides may be sprinkled .But the root is hidden. The existence of the tree depends on the root not on the branches and leaves. Hence the roots have their own needs. That needs ought to be understood and taken care of.

We the human beings have 'Locus of Control'. It means the source of our response to any thought, actions, sayings or any object etc. It may be classified as External and Internal. Most of the time we are governed by the external ones such as –

- Opinion of the people
- Past events

- Happening around
- Others observation

Opinion of the people is important as long as it is constructive and helpful in tracing out the shortcomings. But unfortunately our society has paid heavily because of this. We in social affair, suffer from LKK syndrome (Log Kiya Kahenge). Following this we have made our marriages and other important social event a mega event. Of late we have started associating this with social status. And have-nots have terribly been at the receiving end. Dotation started and cases of dowry went up. Girl child became a burden which lead to female foeticide. Now people who had daughters, justified amassing wealth irrespective of the means adopted. In our personal life we try to satisfy everybody which is impossible. We have to realize that we are only responsible for our success and failure. It is rightly said listen to every-one but do whatever your heart tells.

We always remain stuck with the past event and hence can't do justice with the present. We allow past happening to control us. And the moment we do it we have to bear the burden of so many bags of the past. In fact past comes to teach us. If we allow ourselves to be taught by it then our present becomes better and future turns out to be the best. The world has suffered politically and socially a lot because of this. Countries have been fighting for the past-happenings. Races and communities bear hatred and animosity, raking the past.

Whatever happens to us is not under our control but our reaction to the happening is under our control. The impact of the happening depends on the response we give to it. Once Lord Buddha was rebuked by somebody. He smiled and went ahead. His disciple asked the reason of his not reacting. He said, "Whatever that man said, I was not that and therefore I didn't take."

Past comes to teach us. It is, therefore, considered alive. We unfortunately carry bags of the past, which keep pulling us back like an athlete who, while practising, put a heavy rope around him and ties it with a heavy tyre. He needs lots of energy to pull it.

We need to learn how to forget things, happened in the past, that disturbs us today. In a way forgetfulness proves to be a boon in disguise. We don't have to carry its heavy load. If we have patience in the midst of unfavourable situations, created by handful people, it is as if putting our problems before the supreme court(God). The hearing goes in vain before the common people (civil court). But in the supreme court justice may be delayed but never denied.

We need to maintain good relationships. They ought not to be our liabilities but source of encouragement. Good relationships help in creating a positive and creative environment. In such an environment an individual can enjoy their own company.

The second source of responses which are internal and that make us act on the right direction and at the right time. They are vision, dream, will etc.The sooner an individual understands this fact the better they do in life.

THE ESSENCE-

The unsaid epicentre of all the endeavour of human beings is 'Happiness or bliss'. Since most of the us are unaware of how to collect it (happiness), we are ignorant to the art of being happy. The day we learn how to be happy in all ups and downs of life, we learn the greatest skill of life. To be happy is easier than to be sorrowful. But we need to have ideas about the reasons which make us unhappy. The followings may sound logical to you-

i. we can not be happy if we are getting what we don't want and we are not getting what we want.

ii. we can not be happy if most of the time we take interest in others.

iii. we get happiness in distributing it not just by having desire for it.

iv. we can never be happy if we attach big expectations from others.

v. we can not have true happiness if it is conditional.

vi. We can not be happy if we have the habit of stretching things out of proportions.

vii. We can not be happy if we have fault-finding attitude in everything and every actions, performed by people around us.

viii. we can not be happy unless we have flexibility in our approach.

ix. we can not be happy if we are devoid of any work and lack purpose in our life.

In the happiness index of the world, Japan tops in the list. There is an island named, Okinawa' in the south of Japan, where people live longer than people anywhere else in the world. According to the researchers ,people in Japan, especially in the northern a part of the Okinawa island there is a place called Ogimi, a rulral town, which has a unique distinction in having the maximum longevity in the world. Hence the very town is nicknamed as the Village of Longevity.

There is Japanese concept of 'Ikigai' which, to understand easily ,can be translated as 'the happiness of always being busy'.

What surprised the researchers the most is that the place where two hundred thousand innocent lives were deprived from their earthly life in one go during the second world war, was setting example for the rest of the world by having people who were the happiest, resulting in their maximum longevity in the world and this ,they have made possible by following the principle of 'ichariba chode', a local expression which means "treat everyone like a brother, even if you've never met them before".

Life oughtn't be devoid of purpose, not in the layman sense of making ones living, having luxuries for family and decent success according to the society, but the work (purpose) that keeps you active. And there is no retirement in it. You don't get tired of doing that. This varies person to person.

According to the Japanese, everyone has an 'ikigai'-what has also been termed as 'raison d'etre'(reason for being, the claimed reason for the existence of something or someone). Some people find and lead a blessed life. But most of the people keep searching it through out their life. However successful they are in their life. Consequently they have to lead an unhappy life. Their search ends with life. The amount of counselling and search we do to opt our career or decide our aim of life, a little effort is also required to trace out the hidden passion we have. It will have multi dimensions. Whichever we find viable we can go for it.

In the general proceedings of the world every goal or aim has a certain stipulated time span and therefore has a time for retirement. After that we are not entertained there. We are officially declared superannuated, which means, obsolete or out of date. In some cases the very feeling of not being fit for work (officially), however mentally and physically sound we may be, catapult us in the state of depression and disappointment. Especially when the difference, in the behaviour of the people around, is perceptible. In such a state of affair if we have a purpose of life : ikigai in the Japanese term, we can insulate ourselves from all the negative emotions. It will prove to be a post-retirement-backup-plan and may help in resisting the mental and physical erosion that takes place due to ageing.

Today what seems to be sporadic in other countries ,the same is the hall mark of Japanese people i.e the sense of community. It makes them stay active throughout their life as it gives them purpose that guides them, keeping pace with the ups and down of life. The very purpose manifests in the actions that prove to be useful for themselves and for the community at large. People engage themselves in the community service. Gavin Bradely says, "Metabolism slows down 90 percent after 30 minutes of sitting. The enzymes that moves the bad fat from our arteries to our muscles, where it can get burnt off, slow down. And after two hours, good cholesterol drops 20 percent."

The greatest gift of the modern science and technology to the world is sedentary life style, wrapped in the packet of advancement. We can find ways to deal with the situations. Ways such as-at least twenty minutes walk every day, participate in social activities ,may be some sports or any activity which involves movement of the body, avoid Hurry, Worry and Curry as all these lead to the steps of the hospitals ,consider sleep to be the most precious gift of god, use it judiciously, keep observing the response of our body, It will help us to trace out the harmful habits, consequently we can bring about changes in our routine to make our body and mind at ease with the existing situations.

At the outset of my teaching career, I could only relate the situations, that I had experienced as a student and above all as a son of a dedicated teacher. But, as every inning is a new inning, so is the experience of life, especially when there have been innumerable changes in all different departments of education. The most important one is certainly the mind-set of the students as they are, day in and day out, getting exposed to the most updated knowledge through internet. Ideas are becoming obsolete in great pace.

In such a mind boggling state for the young generation where they frequently come across contradicting ideas, it becomes difficult for them to stick to the right and viable one (idea). According to a research the span of 'generation gap' has reduced to mere six years. It means, six years difference in age, senior or junior, is next generation or last generation. They are emotionally or even physically fragile because of the over protection given at every step by their parents and unsuitable dietary habits. They need to be told the values, upheld by our fathers and forefathers while nurturing us. They need to be given spiritual insulation to resist the temptation of glittering artificiality, in the garb of advancement and modernisation. And this is only possible when an atmosphere is created wherein they get to witness how relationships are valued and elders' concerns (understood as interference by many in this technically and philosophically advanced world) are acknowledged, respected and appreciated.

After having taught for more than twenty years, I can say with full responsibility that our education system, which is knowledge based, doesn't have the elements for character building. Much depends on the parental guidance, for the students being socially and morally awaken individual, to be building block of the country. Parents ought not to be hell bent on making them a money minting machine. They should not be the source of their bank balance but a good source of happiness and social balance.

Today after weathering harshness of different seasons for twenty years I sit in the middle of a school classroom I realize, how world is a classroom for all of us and time is a teacher which teaches us after taking our test. Perhaps this is how every-one gets to bat on a different wicket. I got what I was destined to get. Now I feel, without the element of repentance, that I could have used each day as a fresh ball bowled by bowler on the wicket one has to bat only, without getting stuck to the ball missed or days rolled down, because TIME is always the bowler which keeps bowling with lots of variations. I am reminded of the famous lines of Robert Frost – But I have promise to keep, miles to go before I sleep, miles to go before I sleep.........................

(1.Ikigai-Hector Gracia and Fransesc Miralles)
(Ikigai   by   Hector   Gracia   and   F.Miralles,page

135,HUTCHINSON LONDON)

www.ingramcontent.com/pod-product-compliance
Lightning Source LLC
Chambersburg PA
CBHW020733160726
47993CB00006B/2424